C.J. Eisenstadt Whitmore

The Bible in the Workshop

A refutation of Bishop Colenso's critical examination of the Pentateuch and the book of Joshua. Second Edition

C.J. Eisenstadt Whitmore

The Bible in the Workshop
A refutation of Bishop Colenso's critical examination of the Pentateuch and the book of Joshua. Second Edition

ISBN/EAN: 9783337105006

Printed in Europe, USA, Canada, Australia, Japan

Cover: Foto ©Lupo / pixelio.de

More available books at **www.hansebooks.com**

From the Library of

Professor William Henry Green

Bequeathed By him to
the Library of

Princeton Theological Seminary

THE BIBLE IN THE WORKSHOP.

THE
BIBLE IN THE WORKSHOP.

A REFUTATION

OF

BISHOP COLENSO'S CRITICAL EXAMINATION OF THE PENTATEUCH AND BOOK OF JOSHUA.

BY TWO WORKING MEN,
A JEW AND A GENTILE.

SECOND EDITION, REVISED.

הֶאֱמַנְתִּי כִּי אֲדַבֵּר
PSALM CXVI.

Γρηγορεῖτε, στήκετε ἐν τῇ πίστει, ἀνδρίζεσθε, κραταιοῦσθε.
PAUL.

LONDON:
W. KENT & CO., PATERNOSTER ROW.

HARRILD, PRINTER, LONDON.

ADVERTISEMENT.

Two Journeymen Mechanics, working for London Firms at their respective trades of Printing and Bookbinding, borrowed a copy of Dr. Colenso's work on the Pentateuch from a City Missionary, and sat down together for a few evenings, after their day's work was done, in order to study carefully what the Bishop had advanced. They have made the following notes of their investigation.

We take the opportunity afforded by a Second Edition to add:—We appreciate the compliment implied in the doubt so often expressed, that this Refutation has been written by Journeymen Mechanics; but neither the Publishers nor ourselves would consent to any deception. Every word has been written by one workman; with the advice and assistance of the other, in all matters concerning Jewish customs and the Hebrew language.

PREFACE.

The first circumstance that forced itself upon our attention was the strange position in which we were placed. We had been accustomed to look upon Bishops, Priests, and Deacons, as well as Dissenting Ministers, as, professionally, strenuous and constant advocates of the truth and authority of the Holy Scriptures. It had never happened within our experience that a Bishop of the Church of England had "written a book" coolly avowing his belief that the Scriptures were "fables," not even "cunningly devised." We had both repeatedly heard such assertions at Infidel Lectures, where, of course, we had expected nothing else; but to find ourselves in companionship with a volume written by a Bishop, containing the same arguments we had often listened to at the Infidel Lecture Hall, was a new and very unpleasant experience. It was not less unpleasant to read on the placards of the same Infidel Lecture Hall, that extracts from the Bishop's Book were to be read on Sunday Evening before the usual Lecture, when the favourite orator being absent, it was feared that the funds would suffer, and the Bishop's work was selected to make up for the usual amount of blasphemous ribaldry. Thus to have a Bishop of the English Church claimed as an exponent of infidelity was as new as it was disagreeable, and we will here thank the Bishop of Natal for making Christian men in workshops the jibe and sport of the profane and unbelieving; for strengthening the hands of infidels and atheists in a manner and to a degree that the most sanguine amongst their number had scarcely dared to hope for, and for weakening the efforts and discouraging the minds of earnest Christian working men in exactly the same proportion.

And with what design ? we have wonderingly asked ourselves since attentively reading the Bishop's volume. What purpose of truth or usefulness could the Bishop hope to serve by issuing such a compilation ? He is supposed to be a minister of Christ. Did he expect to advance our Lord's kingdom by, at least, insinuating that He was liable to human error ? He is supposed to exercise himself in the Holy Scriptures ; but the Bishop says one thing and the Book of Psalms asserts the contrary as plainly as it is possible to do so—as we have shown (p. 45) ; and to "build us up in the comfort of our most holy faith," by doing his best to undermine and destroy our belief in the Mosaic Narrative upon which all that faith is completely dependent, is a new and most uncomfortable way for a chief shepherd to feed the Master's sheep.

There is, however, no lack of avowal on the part of the Bishop of what he intends to do if he is able. There is no attempt to disguise the uncompromising hostility of his criticism upon the first six books of the Holy Scriptures. He does not leave the slightest doubt upon the mind of the reader that he intends to prove, if he can, the untruthfulness of the Pentateuch, or, as he himself terms it, the unhistorical character of those books. But why not speak out plainly ? If they are unhistorical, they are but a collection of fables, pure and simple, and the sooner they become the companions of "Jack, the Giant-killer," the better. There can be no positive teaching drawn from a book, in which it requires a close study to detect the hidden fable from the hidden truth ; and the whole history is either one of gross imposture, unworthy the notice of men living in earnest, or it is part of the oracles of the living God.

But the Bishop will not endorse this view of the subject ; he tells us the books are unhistorical, but written without any culpable intention to deceive—see Colenso's Preface, p. xvii., note, where we read the following rich sentence :—" It is *we* who do *him* (the writer of the story of the Exodus) wrong, and do wrong to the excellence of the Scripture story by maintaining that it must be historically true, and that the writer *meant* it to be received and believed as such." So that while the writer of the Pentateuch endeavours to give every possible proof of truthfulness, and has succeeded so well as to make thousands of clear and powerful minds believe not only that he meant to write truth, but that he really accomplished his object; the Bishop of Natal informs us that it is all a mistake, and that the Pentateuch to be in its right place, must be classed with the " Pilgrim's Progress," the " Death of Abel," and other works of the same character. But Bunyan and Gesner own that their works are allegories. Why is not the author of the " Pentateuch" equally candid and open? To prove the unhistorical character of the Pentateuch, and so inevitably destroy the influence of the Bible on the minds and hearts of Christian men, is the strange employment the Bishop of Natal has proposed to himself, and has done his best to accomplish; and we, two plain working men, beg to ask if this is fitting employment for a Bishop of the Church of England *as such?* He replies that *it is* in one place (Introductory remarks, page 5), and that *it is not* in another (Preface, page 12), and having thus given us an idea of his own consistency, and the authoritative weight we ought to attach to his teachings, he leaves us to settle the question for ourselves.

In his Preface the Bishop fears he will have to leave the Church. In the Introductory Remarks which follow he rejoices to find the necessity removed by the recent decision of the Court of Arches. His retaining his position may be perfectly legal; there are many other *legal* acts which a good and true man would hesitate to perform; but the question to be considered is, not the *legality* but the *honesty* of any course of conduct.

Through an oversight or laxity in ecclesiastical law it may be possible for Dr. Colenso to retain his Bishopric in the Church of England without teaching the doctrines he personally accepted when he was allowed to enter upon his duties and enjoy his emoluments and privileges. But suppose a case: That either of us two working men went to the Bishop and informed him that our employers, having contracted to pay us for our time, had asked us to perform work for which we were disinclined, and which we could not see it right to do. What would the Bishop advise? "If you cannot agree with your employers and work in harmony with them, you had far better leave their establishment." Surely he has voluntarily placed himself in a precisely similar position. If his disagreement with the Establishment he is connected with, is of such a thorough and fundamental character as it appears to be, is he not bound, as an honest straightforward man, to leave it, and seek some other employment? He took office as a Christian Minister on the express, plainly stated contract of his unfeigned belief in the Canonical Scriptures of the Old and New Testament: on no other terms whatever *could* he have been admitted to the ministry of the church; and if (from exceedingly weak and insufficient reasons, as they appear to us) he no longer holds the belief he once assuredly professed, he can no longer conscientiously enjoy the rights, privileges, and emoluments depending thereupon. Inasmuch as, no longer believing in the truth and authority of the Canonical Scriptures of the Old Testament, he cannot expound them and enforce their belief on other persons; neither can he honestly withhold the privileges and emoluments from some other person, who is in a condition to fulfil the contract, upon which they were, and are still, granted from the Church Establishment.

What can the Bishop of Natal *do* or *teach* NOW? He cannot teach that the Bible is the Truth of God; he cannot avouch that the Pentateuch is historically correct. He must, to be consistent, own that he believes the Lord Jesus Christ was liable to human error, and inasmuch as Our Blessed Lord repeatedly (in more than a dozen instances) stakes His character and His knowledge on the truth of the Books which the Bishop declares to be untrue, the Bishop can no longer consistently teach the doctrine of the Divinity of our Lord and Saviour. What, then, remains for him to teach that the church to which he is attached, can and will accept as *quid pro quo?*

If no satisfactory answer be given to these plain and straightforward questions, however legal the Bishop's position may be, common honesty appears to us to demand that he should at once resign a position where all the advantage is on one side; to retain the salary with the duties unperformed, or to receive emoluments while refusing to render the services stipulated for in return, are not the acts of an honest man.

The Bishop can still teach the doctrine of Intuitive Religion; but surely this does not exist amongst the Formularies of the Church of England. He can teach that mankind are independent alike of Inspiration and Revelation; but if such doctrines are truths,—if the innate religion of the Sikh Gooroo whom the Bishop has taken for his Model, is as valuable and authoritative as Christianity, then also the intuition of the Zulu heathen must be as truthful and beneficial as that of his Christian Bishop (whatever that may be); all necessity for bishops and bishoprics is at once at an end, and Bishop Colenso's ministrations in his diocese are unnecessary and impertinent.

Nor need it be considered strange, if while at the end of his first part the Bishop becomes enthusiastic in praise of his new Gooroo religion, he never once mentions "the Name that is above every name;" that he utterly ignores the teaching, and person, and work of the Lord Jesus Christ. He mentions a God of Truth, and avers Him revealed to us in an untruthful revelation. We are to be Christians without Christ, saved without a Saviour, redeemed from our lost and ruined condition without a Redeemer, taught by a mistaken Teacher, instead of a Leader, authorized, truthful, and divine; we are to be relegated to the dominion of a seared conscience, and a deceitful and desperately wicked heart, and to have such a chance of getting to heaven at last as these will leave us; our only warrant for believing in the existence of such a place at all being contained in a book stigmatized as untruthful, and consequently not to be trusted.

Nor is this all, the Bishop in depriving us of our support and stay, forces back upon us the sorrowful doubt of the existence of our loved and lost; for certainly (if Christ could be the mistaken one of the Bishop's wild, illogical, cruel, and blasphemous dreamings), "they that are fallen asleep in Christ are perished," and "we are of all men most miserable." Deluded and mistaken in our most sacred and cherished hopes, it were better to be the Bishop's paraded and praised Gooroo than an earnest, striving, Christian Englishman.

For the question is not, as the Bishop falteringly hints it, "Why should it be thought that He (Jesus) would speak with certain *divine* knowledge on this matter?" The question raised is of far more momentous and terrible significance to all that truly believe in Christ. If Jesus Christ *could* be mistaken in his estimate of the Pentateuch, what warrant have we for trusting any portion of His teaching as authoritative and divine? what security have we in accepting as trustworthy anything that He said? Our most glorious hope, our highest aspiration, to stand "complete in Him," cannot possibly be fulfilled if He were incomplete in Himself. We humbly but reverently thank our God that the Scriptures (in the belief of which the Bishop's book has not the least disturbed us) expressly declare that "in Him dwelleth all the fulness of the Godhead bodily," and (matchless declaration of goodness and truth), .that "we are complete in Him."

The Bishop asks concerning Jesus, "At what period then, of his life on earth is it to be supposed that He had granted to Him, as the Son of Man, *supernaturally,* full and accurate information on these points, so that He should be expected to speak about the Pentateuch in other terms than any devout Jew of that day would have employed?" The fact being, that the testimony of Our Lord in favour of the Pentateuch is so emphatic, so utterly irreconcileable with the Bishop's theory, that as the testimony cannot, the *value* of it must be destroyed. We will simply answer the Bishop's question by reverently pointing out to him, that *all the Lord Jesus Christ is now,* is responsible for our belief in the truth of the Pentateuch, because after He had risen from the dead, He emphatically repeated the truths He had before asserted on this subject, *i.e.,* that Moses was a prophet, and that the books were his writing, when, "beginning at Moses and all the prophets, He expounded unto them in all the Scriptures the things concerning Himself," Luke xxiv. 27. So that the Bishop's supposition involves the awful consequence, that the teaching of our Lord on the most important of all subjects, his own divinity, after He rose from the dead, was erroneous and mistaken.

One other point and we quit this saddening subject. The Bishop says the Pentateuch is unhistorical, consequently untrue: and we will, therefore, draw attention to the fact that in our Lord's Temptations in the Wilderness all three of the quotations He used to baffle the Evil One, are taken from the Pentateuch; so that our Lord achieved a victory over the Father of Lies by quoting a book that was, itself, untruthful. We feel that we need only point out the circumstances, and that any comment is unnecessary.

Now in passing to the consideration of every difficulty the Bishop has put forth, we intend simply to accept the invitation of the Bishop, and, as far as possible, enter into the most minute detail. We shall confine ourselves to the subjects the Bishop has chosen, leaving aside the vast mass of affirmative evidence which true and honest criticism would have stated and weighed; and we shall try, in our own plain vernacular, to point out the Bishop's weaknesses and errors; and—though we should utterly fail in answering any of his objections—yet decline to follow him into unbelief, until the affirmative evidence has been subjected to the process the Bishop has employed upon the texts upon which his learning and ability have been so misplaced; for (thus writes a great and good man belonging to the same ecclesiastical corporation as the Bishop of Natal himself), "he that with an honest and sincere desire to find out the truth or falsehood of a revelation, inquires into it, *should first consider impartially what can be alleged for it, and* AFTERWARDS *consider the objections raised against it*, that so he may compare the arguments in proof of it, and the objections together; to insist upon particular objections collected out of difficult places of Scripture, without attending to the inner grounds and motions which induce a belief of the truth of the Scripture, is a very fallacious mode of arguing, because it is not in the least improbable that there may be a true revelation which may have great difficulties in it." And if this is the proper course to be taken to arrive at truth, it is also an exact description of that which the Bishop of Natal has certainly *not* done.

The plan we shall adopt in dealing with the Bishop's objections will be, to take his own chapters one after the other, quote the texts upon which the objections are founded, state the objections in the Bishop's own words, and answer them to the best of our ability and research.

CHAPTER I.

Of the Bishop's Book is headed INTRODUCTORY REMARKS, many of which have been noticed in our preface; we shall therefore pass on to consider the first objection in the book.

"CHAPTER II.

"THE FAMILY OF JUDAH." And the quotation made as follows:—"*And the sons of Judah; Er, and Onan, and Shelah, and Pharez, and Zarah: but Er and Onan died in the land of Canaan; and the sons of Pharez were Hezron and Hamul,*" Gen. xlvi. 12.

This is the first text the Bishop wishes to subject to examination, and in the quotation, as above, the word "were" is omitted in the Bishop's book. It may appear ungenerous to say that this was done designedly, and not giving Dr. Colenso credit for the common sense of supposing that the error would be immediately pointed out; but the word "were," there omitted, has been often used to point out the probability that Hezron and Hamul were born after the families of Israel came into Egypt; while the Bishop proceeds to say, "It appears to me to be certain that the writer here means to say that Hezron and Hamul were born in the land of Canaan, and were amongst the seventy persons (including Jacob himself and Joseph and his two sons) who *came into Egypt* with Jacob." Here is the Bishop's objection: "Judah was forty-two years old when Jacob went down into Egypt." "Judah was twenty years of age when he married; he has separately three sons, the oldest grows up, is married, and dies; the second grows up (suppose in another year), marries his brother's widow, and dies; the third grows up (suppose in another year still), but declines to take his brother's widow to wife." [If this is criticism, it is of a very loose character, there is no mention of anything of the kind in Genesis.] "She then deceives Judah himself, conceives by him, and in due time bears him twins, Pharez and Zarah. One of these twins also grows to maturity and has two sons, Hezron and Hamul, born to him before Jacob goes down into Egypt." And the Bishop sums up concerning the whole—"Certainly incredible!"

We copy the following from Rogers's "Reason and Faith," thinking that it very ably sets forth a principle here required:— "If an objection be founded on the alleged *absolute* contradiction of two statements, it is quite sufficient to show *any* (not the real, but only a hypothetical and possible,) medium of reconciling them, and the objection in all fairness is dissolved, and this would be felt by the honest logician, even if we did not know of such instances; we do, however, know of many."

Acting on this principle, we suggest the following hypothesis as sufficiently meeting the difficulty.

Genesis xxxviii. 1, says in the Hebrew בָּעֵת הַהִוא "in that time," translated in the English version, "at that time," and understood by the Bishop to mean at the time of the events of the preceding chapter, but taken by the Rabbins in very ancient times to include the whole of the time between the return of Jacob to Canaan and the descent into Egypt, so that it is at least possible, the marriage of Judah took place when he was fourteen years of age. Let us simply suppose he did marry at that age, and then continue our hypothesis from that starting point.

Judah married at fourteen; Er born, Judah fifteen; Onan born, Judah sixteen. Er married at the same age as Ahaz the father of Hezekiah (*i. e.*, ten years of age) or allow one year more, eleven, Judah twenty-six. Er died, Onan married and died, and Tamar, deceiving her father-in-law, but legal husband (say two years), Judah twenty-eight. Pharez and Zarah (twins) born, Judah twenty-nine. Pharez grew up and married at eleven years of age, Judah forty. Hezron born first year, Judah forty-one; Hamul in the second year, Judah forty-two years of age; and yet the Bishop has the hardihood to assert, "certainly incredible." It may with truth be said that we have taken the shortest possible dates; and this is admitted; but to invalidate them it must be shown, not that they are the *shortest possible*, but that they are *impossible;* and until this is done, our hypothesis is a complete and sufficient solution of this first difficulty of Dr. Colenso.

But we could easily have obtained more time had it been needed, for Dr. Colenso falls into a second error at the end of his calculation of the age of Judah, as he fell into the first at his commencement. He says that Jacob came into Egypt in the second year of the famine. This can hardly be possible; it was in that year that Joseph made himself known to his brethren, but it is asserting too much to say that Jacob came into Egypt the same year; the second year of the famine was Joseph's thirty-ninth year, the forty-second of Judah, and we may well allow one year, or even two, for the preparations and actual journey of Jacob and all his household into Egypt.

Thus, then, for the Bishop's first difficulty there are two independent and satisfactory modes of solution, neither of which are "incredible" or impossible, or even improbable.

CHAPTER III.

Is devoted to the Explanations of Commentators, respecting the subject of the previous chapter, and the Bishop's opinions upon them, with which we have nothing to do.

"CHAPTER IV.

"THE SIZE OF THE COURT OF THE TABERNACLE COMPARED WITH THE NUMBER OF THE CONGREGATION." Quotation:— "*Jehovah spake unto Moses, saying, Gather thou the congregation together unto the door of the tabernacle of the congregation. And Moses did as Jehovah commanded him, and the assembly was gathered at the door of the tabernacle of the congregation.*"—Lev. viii. 14. (This second scripture is also wrongly quoted, these are parts of the first, third, and fourth verses.)

The Bishop's objection follows:—" The whole congregation must have consisted of at least 600,000 persons, probably many more, and they were to be gathered unto the door of the Tabernacle, or in a width of 18 feet, where there would be room for nine men only to stand in each row, and where, when so standing, they would have formed the commencement of a line 20 miles in length." Such a length being certainly impossible for all practical purposes, the Bishop takes as proof of the unhistorical character of the narrative. The Bishop then quotes a number of texts to prove that the whole congregation meant every man, woman, and child among the "thousands of Israel." There is no doubt that "all the congregation," included every man, woman, and child in it; but it is singular that the word " all" in English, and כל in Hebrew is the very word that is omitted in the text the Bishop has chosen, to prove they were *all* commanded to meet there; nor has the Bishop cited a single text where *all* the congregation are commanded to assemble at the same time. But the Bishop insists on the literal reading that all the congregation shall include nothing less than every man, woman, and child in Israel. We will take two of the instances he has quoted, and see what his literal rendering will make of them.

The first is the stoning of the blasphemer, Lev. xxiv. 14. "Bring forth him that hath cursed without the camp, ... and let *all* the congregation stone him." So every one of the two millions of the congregation, men and women and little children took each of them a separate stone, and one after the other cast it upon him until he died! Again, in the case of the Sabbath-breaker (Num. xv. 36), "all the congregation brought him without the camp, and stoned him with stones until he died;" that is, reading literally, the man had from two to four millions of hands laid upon him, dragging or pushing him along, and then two millions of stones cast separately upon him until he died. This is reading literally; the plain simple meaning in this case, as in all the others, being, a general assembly acting in the name of, and considered as, the whole congregation. But if we are to read literally, let us take a literal reading from Bishop Colenso's own book, p. 40, lines 13, 14 :—" We have to imagine the priest having *himself to carry on his back* (the italics are ours) on foot, from St. Paul's to the outskirts of the metropolis." Making the usual allowance, and finishing the quotation, the bishop's *meaning* is perfectly plain, but in the example we have quoted, we have only acted toward the Bishop, as he has toward the Bible, taking what suited our purpose, and leaving out the remainder of the paragraph as he has left out the second part of a verse. (See p. 28.)

"CHAPTER V.

"MOSES AND JOSHUA ADDRESSING ALL ISRAEL." Quotation: "*These be the words which Moses spake unto all Israel*," Deut. i. 1. "*And Moses called all Israel and said unto them,*" Deut. v. 1. "*And afterward he read all the words of the law, the blessings and the cursings, according to all which is written in the book of the law.*

There was not a word of all that Moses commanded which Joshua read not before all the congregation of Israel, with the women, and the little ones, and the strangers that were conversant among them."
—Josh. viii. 34, 35.

The Bishop's objection follows. "The Israelites numbered certainly over two millions; how, then, is it conceivable that a man should do what Joshua is here said to have done. We must suppose that at least the great body of the congregation was present, and not only present, but able to hear the words of awful moment which Joshua addressed to them. Nor can it be supposed that he read them, first to one party, and then to another, till all the congregation had heard them. The day would not have sufficed to read in this way all the blessings and all the cursings in Deut. xxvii. and xxviii., much less all the words of the law many times over, especially as he had been already engaged, as the story implies, on the very same day, in writing a copy of the law of Moses upon the stones set up in Mount Ebal."

We can find nothing whatever in the Narrative upon which to base these several objections to its truthfulness. We have seen in the chapter immediately foregoing, that the whole congregation could and would, for all practical purposes, have met together when a general promiscuous body of them were in public meeting assembled, with power to act in the name of those present and absent. The statement that Joshua could not be heard by all the people at once, is simply a repetition of the literal reading of the former passage, and it is nowhere asserted that he spoke to all the children of Israel, strangers, etc., at one time. The Bishop says, "it cannot be supposed he addressed them in different divisions;" but he should have given us some proof, for the assertion to carry any weight. Nor would, says the Bishop, one day have sufficed to write the law, and afterwards read it many times over. This may be very freely admitted, for there is not the slightest hint in the Narrative whether these transactions occupied a day, a week, or a month. The objections in these two last chapters are worse than trivial, they are wasteful alike of time and patience. The Bishop should have remembered, that an objection to carry convincing weight, should be founded on a clear assertion of the Scripture Narrative, not have its sole origin in the imagination of the objector. The statement that all this is said or even implied to have taken place on one day, is either a gross and unpardonably careless blunder, disgraceful and fatal to any pretensions to critical examination, or it is something inconceivably worse.

"CHAPTER VI.

"THE EXTENT OF THE CAMP COMPARED WITH THE PRIESTS' DUTIES AND THE DAILY NECESSITIES OF THE PEOPLE." Quotation:—"*The skin of the bullock and all his flesh, with his head, and with his legs, and his inwards, and his dung, even the whole bullock shall he (the priest) carry forth without the camp unto a clean place, where the ashes are poured out, and burn him on the wood with fire, where the ashes are poured out shall he be burnt.*" —Lev. iv. 11, 12.

In this chapter of a book he entitles a "Critical Examination," the Bishop has committed himself to the following passage:— "We have to imagine the priest having himself to carry on his back on foot, from St. Paul's, to the outskirts of the Metropolis, the skin and flesh, head and legs, inwards and dung, even the whole bullock;" and, by way of climax, the Bishop adds, "Further, we have to imagine half a million of men going out daily—

the 22,000 Levites for a distance of *six miles*—to the suburbs for the common necessities of nature."

We now must see what all this is founded on, and it is as follows. "The whole population at the Exodus was 2,000,000, four square yards allowed for each, 8,000,000 yards, or more than 1652 acres of ground. We must imagine a vast encampment of this extent, swarming with people, more than a mile and a-half across in each direction, with the tabernacle in the centre. They could not surely have all gone outside the camp for the necessities of nature."

In answer to this, we assert, "there is no command anywhere in the Bible for any man, woman, or child, to leave the Camp in the Wilderness for any such purpose." There is a direction as to what is to be done by warriors, when campaigning, after the entrance of the Israelites into Canaan, and this one occurs among them. (Comp. Deut. xix. 1, with xxiii. 12—14.)

The Bishop's next objection is, that there would be no wood for fuel; he surely cannot be ignorant of the custom in the desert of using animal dung for that purpose.

But the main objections of this chapter are, that the extent of the camp rendered it impossible for the priest to perform the duties required of him, and for the scavengers of the camp to perform theirs. The Bishop says, "the camp was more than a mile and a half across in each direction, or three square miles in the whole;" and then proceeds to argue his point as though the outside of the camp was beyond this distance, and that the priest had to carry the bullock accordingly. It is difficult to imagine that this is anything else but culpable dishonesty and misrepresentation when we find the Bishop saying, on p. 41, there was *one* camp, and on p. 43 (one single leaf of his book only turned over), that there were *four* camps, and not even then including the central camp of the Levites. In p. 41 it suits the

Bishop's purpose to speak of it as one camp; on p. 43 the numbers inhabiting the east, west, north, and south camps are expressly stated. If, then, there were (including the camp of the Levites) five separate and distinct camps within three square miles, as we have it on the Bishop's own authority, what becomes of his imaginary picture of the priest carrying the bullock six miles, and of his other imagining, of the Levites travelling the same distance for the common necessities of nature? Cheerfully allowing the twelve square miles of Scott for the whole congregation of 2,000,000, the census of the Levites being only in round numbers 20,000, their camp would only occupy the hundredth part of the twelve miles; or, to put it in other words, instead of the priests and Levites having to walk six miles with the offerings, about one hundred yards would be the distance they were required to traverse in carrying the sacrifices.

As to the priest carrying the bullock on his back on foot, it will be quite time enough to occupy ourselves with such a question when we find anything of the kind stated anywhere else than in the Bishop's "Critical Examination." There is not a single word in the Narrative to show that one priest might not carry the skin (upon a cart or otherwise), another priest the head, another the legs, and so on, for as many journeys or persons as might be required; indeed, it appears to us that the bullock *must* have been cut up, or why mention first, particulars, as head, legs, inwards, etc., and afterwards state the whole bullock? The Bishop takes this to mean that the bullock was to be in one piece; to us it appears simply to intimate that no portion was to be left behind for the priests' use as food, which was allowed in the case of other offerings. "The supposition" (concludes the Bishop) "involves, of course, an absurdity. But it is our duty to look plain facts in the face." Doubtless the supposition involves an absurdity, and one of the plain facts we have to look in the face is, that of the Bishop inventing such an absurdity, and then attempting to fasten it upon the Holy Scriptures; and a second plain fact to be looked in the face is, the fitness of such occupation for a Bishop of the Church of England.

"CHAPTER VII.

"THE NUMBER OF THE PEOPLE AT THE FIRST MUSTER, COMPARED WITH THE POLL-TAX RAISED SIX MONTHS PREVIOUSLY." Quotation:—"*And Jehovah spake unto Moses, saying, When thou takest the sum of the children of Israel, after their number, then shall they give every man a ransom for his soul unto Jehovah when thou numberest them. This they shall give every one that passeth among them that are numbered, half a shekel, after the shekel of the sanctuary, an half shekel shall be the offering of Jehovah.*"— Exod. xxx. 11—13.

"We may first notice," says the Bishop, "that the expression 'shekel of the sanctuary,' in the above passage, could hardly have been used in this way until there was a sanctuary, here it is used six or seven months before the tabernacle was made. The LXX., indeed, render the Hebrew phrase by τὸ δίδραχμον τὸ ἅγιον, the sacred shekel. But this can hardly be the true meaning of the original, בְּשֶׁקֶל הַקֹּדֶשׁ; and if it were, the difficulty would still remain, to explain what the 'sacred shekel' could mean before any sacred system was established."

In answering this objection we may simply say that if the Bishop had looked in Gesenius, he would have seen the true rendering of the above Hebrew words (shekel hakkodesh), the *holy* shekel, and that it is thus distinguished from the *royal* shekel afterwards mentioned in 2 Sam. xiv. 26. Any Jewish child could have told him the root word קָדוֹשׁ meant "holy,"

and might very possibly have asked him if he had never heard of
יְרוּשָׁלַיִם הַקְּדוֹשָׁה (Jerusalem the holy).

Passing from the shekel to the numbering of the people, the direction is that every one that is numbered shall pay half a shekel. In Ex. xxxviii. 26 the money is paid, but no census taken. In Num. i., 1—46 the census is taken, but no money mentioned; but the reckoning of the money at one time and the number of persons at another proves that the numbers at the different periods were identical; and, says the Bishop, "It is surprising that the number of adult males should have been identically the same (603,556) on the first occasion as it was half-a-year afterwards."

As in the Bishop's first difficulty, so in this; there are two separate and independent ways of meeting and dissolving it. Michaelis says that the money and numbers are two parts of a whole, recorded in different places. In Exodus, he says, there is no account of a numbering, but every one who was more than twenty years old, paid his tax, and was registered accordingly, but in Numbers Moses received instructions to arrange the lists and sum them up. We may add to this that the translation in the margin (Ex. xxx. 12) points very distinctly to a numbering in connection with the atonement money. But it is evident that this answer is not entirely satisfactory, inasmuch as the atonement money had been collected and appropriated to the building of the tabernacle, and it was in the tabernacle itself that the second commandment was given, so that we must allow the very great probability of the two different numberings, in fact, that there were two entirely different numberings, and that the results were identical. What, in that case, are we required to believe? Simply that, during that period of six months *just as many Israelites reached twenty years of age as died beyond that period.* In other words, that at the end of six months the number of the population remained stationary. "Surprising!" is the comment of the Christian

Bishop; but, as he neither adds nor asserts anything more, we may safely follow the same course, only pointing out that, though it may be a very singular coincidence, it is neither impossible or incredible.

"CHAPTER VIII.

"THE ISRAELITES DWELLING IN TENTS." Quotation: "*Take ye every man for them which are in his tents.*"—Ex. xvi. 16.

The Bishop remarks: "Here we find that immediately after their coming out of Egypt, the people were provided with *tents*—cumbrous articles to have carried when they fled out in haste, taking their dough before it was leavened, their kneading troughs being bound up in their clothes upon their shoulders. It is true this statement conflicts strangely with that in Lev. xxiii. 42, 43, where it is assigned as a reason for their 'dwelling in booths' for seven days at the Feast of Tabernacles, that 'your generations may know that I made the children of Israel to dwell in *booths* when I brought them out of the land of Egypt.' It cannot be said that the word 'booths' here means 'tents'; because the Hebrew word for a *booth* made of *boughs* and bushes סֻכָּה, which is the word here used,* is quite different from that for a tent, אֹהֶל used in Ex. xvi. 16. And besides, in the context of the passage in Leviticus, we have a description of the way in which these booths were to be made, Ye shall take you the boughs of goodly trees, branches of palm trees, and the boughs of thick trees and willows of the brook (ver. 40). This seems to fix the meaning of the Hebrew word in this particular passage, and to show that

---

* Will the Bishop kindly inform us in what edition of the Hebrew Bible this word occurs in the passage quoted? We have searched Van der Hooght, Simonis, Boothroyd, Bagster, the American, the Jews' Society, and the Unpointed Hebrew, and it is not in any one of them.

it is used in its proper sense of booths; though in 2 Sam. xi. 11, and one or two other places, it is also used improperly for tents."

We have quoted this long passage with the intention of exhibiting the remarkable depth and profundity of the criticism here applied to the Holy Scriptures. In this one paragraph the Bishop first asserts that the statement that they had *tents* conflicts strangely with the statement that they dwelt in *booths*, and then proceeds to show that the words can be used interchangeably, and actually points out instances where they are placed the one for the other. But we will look further at the contrast stated by the Bishop to exist between *tents* and *booths*. In Amos ix. 11, the tabernacle or house of David, is described as אֶת־סֻכַּת דָּוִיד; in Isa. xvi. 5, the tabernacle or "house" of David, is described as אֹהֶל דָּוִד; again, אֹהֶל is used to describe the tabernacle, 1 Kings i. 39; the temple, Ezek. xli. 1; and also a house or habitation of any kind, as in Jer. iv. 20; Lam. ii. 4; so that אֹהֶל may mean any kind of human habitation, from the glorious Temple, to the meanest rag spread over a pole, beneath which humanity has ever crawled to die; and סֻכָּה is used to describe a tent hung with curtains, Lev. xxiii. 43 (Ges. Lex. p. 585); a small ruined house, Amos ix. 11; and סֻכִּיִּים (Sukkiim), 2 Chron. xii. 3, is translated by Gesenius, "dwellers in *tents*." Moreover, Jonah constructed סֻכָּה for himself of such a slight and fragile description, that it needed the added shelter of the gourd to keep him from being exposed to the rays of the sun as he sat watching for the fulfilment of the doom he had pronounced upon the devoted city.

But the Bishop says that סֻכָּה means booths only, as shown in Lev. xxiii. 40, where the command to take boughs of goodly trees, etc., is given, and, as the Bishop expressly states, these boughs were to make booths with; in the Narrative quoted, there is not one word of the kind, but expressly the contrary, for instead of the boughs being to build booths with, according to the Bishop, we are told in the *same verse of which the Bishop has quoted part;* *and omitted the remainder, which tells against him,* that the boughs were to be used in "rejoicing before the Lord." Not only so, but as will be seen by referring to any English Bible with marginal references, the word translated "*boughs*" in the text (Lev. xxiii. 40), is also translated "*fruit,*" and thus it is commonly understood by the Jews also, so that while we can well imagine the Jews offering their fruits before the Lord, and rejoicing therein, we are not acquainted with any sort of fruit that would serve to build a house with, as the Bishop would render the passage. Surely the Bishop knew the word could be so translated; might he not have had feeling enough for the grand Old Book to have suggested this simple solution of his own difficulty!

But all this in passing; the strength of the Bishop's objection lies in the fact of the *tents* themselves, called by what name soever they may be. He says, in short, that a tent with poles and cords was a load for a bullock, that only ten could decently live in a tent; therefore, 200,000 tents, with 200,000 oxen to carry them were needed. To expose this absurdity it is only necessary to ask the Bishop, how many slaves have escaped by the Underground Railway from the South of America to the North and Canada, and to inquire whether he will not believe that any have escaped, unless we can show that each one had all the comforts of a wealthy and civilized traveller, on every mile of his long and dangerous pilgrimage from Slavery to Freedom.

Where is the assertion found in Exodus that the Israelites had 200,000 tents with poles and cords, each a load for a bullock? Before quitting this subject, however, we will set forth at length one of the translations of the word אֹהֶל, which the Bishop will have was a tent with poles and cords. In 1 Kings viii. 66, there are these words: On the eighth day he sent the people away, and they blessed the king and went unto לְאָהֳלֵיהֶם their tents—"with poles and cords, a load for a bullock"—joyful. It need scarcely be added that as this scene took place after the dedication of the temple, that אֹהֶל here, means the common dwelling houses inhabited by the Israelites after they had obtained possession of the Promised Land.

"CHAPTER IX.

"THE ISRAELITES ARMED." Quotation:—"*The children of Israel went up harnessed out of the land of Egypt.*"—Ex. xiii. 18.

The Bishop states his case as follows: "The word חֲמֻשִׁים, which is here rendered 'harnessed,' appears to mean 'armed,' or 'in battle array,' in all the other passages where it occurs. Thus Josh. i. 14, 'But ye shall pass before your brethren *armed*, all the mighty men of valour, and help them.' So Josh. iv. 12, 'And the children of Reuben, and the children of Gad, and the half tribe of Manasseh, passed over *armed* before the children of Israel, as Moses spake unto them.' And, Jud. vii. 11, 'Then went he down, with Phurah his servant, unto the outside of the armed men that were in the host.' It is possible, also, that the Hebrew word חָשִׁים, which occurs in Num. xxxii. 17, and is rendered 'armed' in the English Version, but which GESENIUS derives from חוּשׁ, 'to make haste,' and renders 'hastening' or in 'haste,' may be also a corruption from חֲמֻשִׁים, by the accidental omission of a letter.

"It is, however, inconceivable that these down-trodden, oppressed people should have been allowed by Pharaoh to possess arms, so as to turn out at a moment's notice 600,000 armed men. But if even in this or any other way they had come to be possessed of arms, is it conceivable that 600,000 armed men in the prime of life would have cried out in ˹panic˼ terror, 'sore afraid' (Ex. xiv. 10), when they saw that they were being pursued?

"The difficulty of believing this has led many commentators to endeavour to explain otherwise, if possible, the meaning of the word. Accordingly in the margin of the English Bible, we find suggested instead of 'harnessed' or 'armed,' in all the above passages except Josh.iv. 12, 'by five in a rank,' because the Hebrew word חֲמֻשִׁים, has a resemblance to חָמֵשׁ, 'five.' And others again explain it to mean 'by fifties,' as the five thousand were arranged in the wilderness of Bethsaida, Mark vi. 40."

We have thus quoted at length the Bishop's argument, because the sequel will show, either that the Bishop's studies in Hebrew are defective, or that he has designedly kept back the truth on this occasion. He has mentioned four instances in which חֲמֻשִׁים occurs, but has not told us that no other instances occur throughout the Bible, as he might have done; of these four instances one is translated "harnessed," and three "armed"; but two out of these three are marked as of doubtful rendering, in the English Version by the addition of "five in a rank" in the margin. Thus then, the whole of this argument must necessarily be built upon a single unchallenged translation of a word. Of the word in Hebrew itself, it may truthfully be said, there is not a more doubtful word in the Old Testament; Gesenius says of it, "The etymology of this word has long been sought for." So that upon a Hebrew word, the etymology of which is unknown, and which, occurring in only four instances, is translated in three different ways, we are to found an argument for the rejection of the Holy Scriptures. This is the state of the case as far as the *pointed* Hebrew Bible is concerned; but if we take up a Hebrew Bible *without points*, or in other words, a much more ancient copy of the Holy Scriptures, we find that the word occurs one hundred and fifty times, thus, חמשים, of which, in the English version, the translation is *once* "harnessed," *three times* "armed," and *one hundred and forty-six times* the common numeral "*fifty*."

If the passages where "harnessed" and "armed" occur, are carefully studied, it will be seen that in these four instances there would be no difficulty, nor any violation of the sense of the context, in substituting "fifty" for either "armed" or "harnessed," at least this rendering would be quite as good, inasmuch as, in one of the instances quoted by the Bishop (Jud. vii. 11), the men said to be "*armed*" are *fast asleep* and one of them at least *dreaming*. Not only so, but if Bishop Colenso had to write down the *word* in Hebrew representing the number "fifty," he must write חמשים, for in no other way could he accomplish that object. Is it not, to say the least, very strange, that the Bishop should utterly ignore these 146 repetitions of the word in dispute, never mentioning it as occurring in the Old Testament at all, never writing it in the Hebrew character, and only incidentally mentioning a translation of it as occurring in the New Testament, Mark vi. 40?

It will not, therefore, be denied, that the foundation for the word, *pointed*, חֲמֻשִׁים is of such a slender description as to be actually worthless for any practical or disputed purpose, and yet the Bishop founds a whole chapter upon it. While, looked upon in that light, it constitutes one-twenty-third portion of the whole of the arguments upon which we are to resign our title of Christians and become disciples of a Gooroo.

But the Bishop avers "the people had arms," and he "wants to know" whence they were procured; for, he continues, "they must have had arms to have fought the Amalekites with, a month afterwards." The Bishop quotes, but dissents from, the explanation of Josephus, *i. e.*, that the Israelites gathered them from the cast-up spoils of the Egyptian warriors who were drowned in the Red Sea; and Josephus conjectured "that this also happened by Divine Providence, that so they might not have been destitute of weapons." But it is not even improbable that, from what they had concealed, what they recovered from the sea, and what few they might rudely fabricate, they became possessed of a small number of arms. Nor must we forget the formidable ox-goad commonly in use among Eastern herdmen,—described by Maundrell as of an extraordinary size. He measured several, and "found them about eight feet long, and at the bigger end about six inches in circumference. They were armed at the lesser end with a sharp prickle for driving the oxen, and at the other end with a small paddle of iron, strong and massy, for cleansing the plough from the clay." In the hand of a powerful man accustomed to its use, such an instrument must be more dangerous and fatal than a sword, and how many thousands of these weapons they had among them we are left to conjecture. But would the Bishop venture to call an enemy furnished with such an instrument an *unarmed* man? "But," says the Bishop, " we must suppose that the *whole body* of 600,000 warriors were armed when they were numbered (Num. 3) under Sinai." We do not see the slightest necessity for the supposition,—there is no foundation for it in the Narrative, and with all the advantages of civilization and warlike appliances in the greatest profusion, we do not think it is true of Englishmen in the present day. The Bishop in concluding this chapter points out the cowardice of the Israelites, and contrasts it with their bravery in the battle with Amalek as a further reason for rejecting the Narrative. Leaving out of the question the strong intimation of miraculous interposition, typified in the held-up hands of Moses; it seems to us, an exquisite touch of nature and of truth, that the released slave should first feel a panic of terror at the hostile appearance of his late tyrant and master, and from the very fact of seeing the only one of whom he had reason to be afraid, rendered powerless to harm him, gather courage to present a brave front before an enemy and a stranger.

"CHAPTER X.

"THE INSTITUTION OF THE PASSOVER." Quotation:—" *Then Moses called for all the elders of Israel, and said unto them, Draw out now, and take you a lamb according to your families, and kill the Passover. And ye shall take a bunch of hyssop, and dip it in the blood that is in the bason, and strike the lintel and the two side posts with the blood that is in the bason, and none of you shall go out at the door of his house until the morning. . . And the children of Israel went away, and did as Jehovah had commanded Moses and Aaron, so did they.*"—Ex. xii. 21—28.

In the first quotation from Scripture the Bishop *left out a word that told against him*, here, the Bishop *puts one in to help him;* the word *now* in the above quotation is not in the Narrative.

The objections are stated by the Bishop in the following paragraphs:—" That is to say, in *one single day* the whole immense population of Israel, as large as that of LONDON, was instructed to keep the Passover, and actually did keep it. I have said 'in one single day,' for the first notice of any such feast to be kept is given in this very chapter, where we find it written (v. 12), 'I will pass through the land of Egypt *this* night, and will smite all the firstborn in the land of Egypt, both man and beast.'

" It cannot be said that they had notice several days beforehand, for they were to '*take*' the lamb on the tenth day of the month, and 'kill' it on the fourteenth, vv. 3, 6; and so v. 12 only means to say 'on *that* night'—the night of the fourteenth—I will pass through the land of Egypt. For the expression in v. 12 is distinctly הַזֶּה, 'this,' not הַהוּא, 'that,' as in xiii. 8, and so v. 14, '*this* day shall be unto you for a memorial;' and, besides, in the chapter preceding (xi. 4) we read, 'And Moses said [to Pharaoh], Thus saith Jehovah, *about midnight* will I go out into

c

the midst of Egypt, and all the firstborn in the land of Egypt shall die,' where there can be no doubt that the midnight then next at hand is intended. It is true that the story as it now stands, with the directions about 'taking' the lamb on the tenth day and 'keeping' it till the fourteenth are perplexing and contradictory. But this is only one of many similar phenomena, which will have to be considered more closely hereafter."

In order that we may thoroughly comprehend and appreciate the mystification in which the Bishop has here either involved himself, or wishes to involve his readers, we will take his assertions on this subject separately, and copied in his own words:—

Assertion 1. "In *one single day* the whole immense population of Israel was instructed to keep the Passover, and actually did keep it."

Assertion 2. "It cannot be said that they had notice several days beforehand."

Assertion 3. "It was absolutely necessary that the notice to keep the Passover should be distinctly given to each separate family."

Assertion 4. "When suddenly summoned to depart, they hastened at a moment's notice to borrow in all directions from the Egyptians."

Assertion 5. "They required 150,000 lambs for the Passover."

Assertion 6. "We are to believe that every single household was warned again at midnight to start at once in hurried flight for the wilderness."

Such are the assertions of the Bishop, stated in his own words; our task is now to ascertain how far they agree with the narrative in Exodus.

Assertion 1. "In one single day" (expressly limited by the Bishop afterward to *twelve hours*) "the Israelites were instructed to keep the Passover, and actually did keep it."

The most convincing and complete refutation of this reckless and unfounded assertion will be to simply quote the English printed text from Ex. xii. 1—6. "And the LORD spake unto Moses and Aaron in the land of Egypt, saying, This month shall be unto you the beginning of months; it shall be the first month of the year to you. Speak ye unto all the congregation of Israel, saying, In the tenth day of this month they shall take to them every man a lamb, according to the house of their fathers; a lamb for an house. And if the household be too little for the lamb, let him and his neighbour next unto his house take it according to the number of the souls; every man according to his eating shall make your count for the lamb. Your lamb shall be without blemish, a male of the first year: ye shall take it out from the sheep, or from the goats. And ye shall keep it up until the fourteenth day of the same month, and the whole assembly of the congregation of Israel shall kill it in the evening" (Heb., as in margin, *between the two evenings*).

The distinct statement here (as it appears to us) is, that God spake to Moses and Aaron on the first day of the month (this is the Jewish tradition, upon which the present Jewish ecclesiastical year is also founded—a strength of proof that no mere assertion will invalidate, let it be made by whom it may), telling them to take the lamb on the tenth day of the month, and "keep it up" "separate by itself" until the fourteenth day of the month. These previous arrangements being undeniable, are stigmatized by the Bishop as "perplexing" and "contradictory:" which they most undoubtedly are to the theory he is advocating, and not only perplexing and contradictory, but utterly destructive also. To make good this first assertion, the Bishop has to overcome this formidable difficulty, *i. e.*, to tell whence the fourteenth of Abib is dated *from*, or, in other words, what is the origin of the present Jewish sacred year, distinguished from the first day of Tisri, the beginning of the Jewish civil year. Until he has done this, we shall take the liberty to say that the Narrative and the commencement of the Jewish sacred year confirm each other in the statement, that, instead of *twelve hours*, at least thirteen days' notice of the Passover was given to all the children of Israel.

Assertion 2. "It cannot be said they had notice several days beforehand."

What, then, is the "perplexing" and "contradictory" order to "keep it up" from the tenth to the fourteenth day of the month, quoted by the Bishop himself from the Narrative? The Bishop has ventured upon one quotation from Josephus in reference to this subject of the Passover (concerning which quotation we have a remark to make), and we will here, make a quotation from the same author which *possibly* the Bishop overlooked:—"But when God had signified that with one more plague he would compel the Egyptians to let the Hebrews go, he commanded Moses to tell the people, that they should have a sacrifice ready, and that they should prepare themselves on the tenth day of the month Xanthicus against the fourteenth;" so that Bishop Colenso and Josephus flatly contradict each other.

Assertion 3. "It was absolutely necessary that the notice to keep the Passover should be distinctly given to each separate family."

Doubtless it was necessary, and there was a sufficient time allowed beforehand for every notice to be given, and for all needed preparation to be made; though, how much of the interval between the first, and tenth of Abib, elapsed before Moses and Aaron made known the commandments they had received, is not stated in the narrative: but that several days' notice were given is proved by Ex. xii. 21, "Then Moses called for all the elders of Israel, and said unto them, Draw out, and take you a lamb according to your families, and kill the Passover." In order that the commandment to "keep up" the lamb should be obeyed, it *must* have been issued, at the very latest, early on the morning of the tenth of Abib.

Assertion 4. "When suddenly summoned to depart, they hastened at a moment's notice to borrow in all directions from the Egyptians."

If the Bishop had ever read attentively and consecutively the Narrative he is commenting on, it seems to us, that he could not have written such a reckless assertion as this. Before there is the slightest hint of the *nature* of the final plague, before a single word is uttered relative to the Passover that was to accompany it; in the interval between the Darkness and the death of the firstborn this commandment is given (Ex. xi. 2, 3), "Speak now in the ears of the people, and let every man borrow of his neighbour, and every woman of her neighbour, jewels of silver and jewels of gold. And the LORD gave the people favour in the sight of the Egyptians." The Septuagint has a word here which is neither in the Hebrew or the English—Δάλησον οὖν ' κρυφῇ' εἰς τά ὦτα·τοῦ λαοῦ, "Speak now 'secretly' in the ears of the people," though the Hebrew used דַּבֶּר־נָא בְּאָזְנֵי הָעָם will certainly bear the same construction. So that the commandment was given and obeyed, and its success recorded, before the slightest hint of the coming Passover is given; and, indeed, the very fact that they would be thrust out hastily is made known, and assigned as a reason why the borrowing should previously take place. This fact of the borrowing is repeated in Ex. xii. 35, 36, and it appears to be this reiteration that has led the Bishop to make the assertion that he has done,—but it ought to have been observed by him that, in the twelfth chapter, only the *obedience to the command* is recorded, we have no account of the *giving* of the commandment, to the children of Israel in that chapter.

Assertion 5. "They required 150,000 lambs for the Passover."

As a very large number of the Bishop's after objections are founded on this statement, it will be necessary to examine the authority upon which it is given. "JOSEPHUS, *De Bell. Jud.*, vi. 9. 3., reckons ten persons on an average for each lamb; but, he says, 'many of us are twenty in a company.' Kurtz allows *fifteen* or *twenty*. Taking ten as the average number, two millions of people would require about 200,000 lambs, taking twenty, they would require 100,000." This is the Bishop's own statement of an objection often reiterated throughout his volume, and we see that *it has not the shadow of a foundation in the narrative in Exodus; no chapter or verse is quoted in support of it, but it is founded on a statement in Josephus, and a mere conjecture of Kurtz.* This very slight and shadowy foundation is *all* the Bishop can show in support of his statement. Against what he has adduced we venture to place the following. Rashi says that "he who has eaten a piece of lamb as large as half an egg has properly observed the Passover," and in the מנן אברהם הלוכות פסח the same regulation is laid down. We will here point out also the unfair mode of dealing with Josephus that is practised in the extract of the Bishop, who says that Josephus reckons ten persons on an average for each lamb, and many of us, he says, are twenty in a company. The words of Josephus are "not less than ten to a lamb, and many of us are twenty in a company," and the Jewish High Priest is speaking of his own time, then present,—more than 1500 years after the time of the narrative in Exodus. In the account he gives of the Passover in Exodus there is not a single word to indicate whether ten persons, or a hundred, or a thousand shared in a Passover lamb. In short, we do not hesitate to assert that the foundation for the Bishop's calculation of the number of lambs required, exists only in his own imagination—neither in the narrative, nor in the parallel passage in Josephus is there the slightest indication upon which such a calculation could be made. There is also another consideration, which must be entered into, before even the most remote approximation to the number of lambs required can be ascertained. The commandment is—a lamb for an house; but a house of what size? How many persons composed the house of David, for instance?—as large as the house known as Knightsbridge Barracks, or as small as the one-roomed cottages down the courts in Clerkenwell. If neither as small as the one or as large as the other, what precise data have we upon which we can rely for certainty? Absolutely none. We have not the remotest idea how many could eat from a single lamb in Egypt,—the number of persons composing the houses is to us equally unknown. It is certain that a very large number of persons *could* have partaken of one lamb; it is equally certain that provision was specially made that a considerable number *should* do so, inasmuch as, if the household were too small for the lamb, the next household was to join in the consumption. The whole of this is the merest generalization: data upon which to make such a calculation as the Bishop has ventured upon, and upon the faith of which he has asserted the untruthfulness of God's Holy Word, is in that Word nowhere to be found. Upon the sole authority of a quotation from Josephus which has not the slightest reference to the time of the Exodus, the Bishop of Natal has dared to impugn the authority of the Holy Scriptures, and to exhibit the mournful spectacle he has thus placed before his indignant, yet sorrowful Christian countrymen.

Assertion 6. "We are to believe that every single household was warned again [the second time during twelve hours] at midnight, to start in hurried flight for the wilderness."

The people were met in solemn conclave (Ex. xii. 11); they knew their long and bitter slavery approached its end, and that their departure should be exceedingly hasty (Ex. xi. 1). They were dressed and ready for flight (Ex. xii. 11), listening intently for the first wild wail of awful and despairing sorrow, that should be at once the signal of deliverance, and the tidings of retributive justice for their own savagely murdered little children (Ex. xi. 5) they waited in intense expectation, for the coming of the angel of Jehovah, every mind wrought to its highest pitch, for they knew that the messenger of the great I AM was commissioned, and ready to execute unquestioningly the awful will of his Master, and that death and desolation would follow swiftly in his train. They were not disappointed; suddenly rang out the hoarse shout of man's unbearable anguish, mingling with the wail of woman's despairing sorrow, and the shrill cry of the terrified Egyptian children—all proclaiming that the promised awful work was done. There was a great cry throughout all the land of Egypt, "for there was not a house where there was not one dead" (Ex. xii. 30). That wild cry was the signal of departure (Ex. xi. 6, 8), and ready dressed, staff in hand, shoes on feet, all things needed obtained beforehand from their oppressors (Ex. xi. 3), in haste, indeed, but jubilant and defiant, from hundreds of years of bitter slavery went forth the people of Him who cannot lie,—they trusted and were not confounded,—God had said it hundreds of years before, and He had done it. Well for *us* if we also trust in the Lord Jehovah, until from the hard bondage of sin and death He shall bring his redeemed ones into the light and splendour of everlasting life, to be with their Father and our Father, and their God and our God, through the death and merit of the Angel of the Everlasting Covenant, our Lord and Saviour Jesus Christ.

"CHAPTER XI.

"THE MARCH OUT OF EGYPT." Quotation:—"*And the children of Israel journeyed from Rameses to Succoth, about six hundred thousand on foot that were men, besides children. And a mixed multitude went up also with them, and flocks and herds, even very much cattle.*"—Ex. xii. 37, 38.

Thus the Bishop states his case :—
"It appears from Num. i. 3, ii. 32, that these 600,000 were the men in the prime of life, from twenty years old and upward, all that were able to go forth to war in Israel. And as we have seen, this large number of able-bodied warriors, implies a total population of at least two millions. Here, then, we have this vast body of people of all ages, summoned to start, according to the story, at a moment's notice, and actually started, not one being left behind, together with all their multitudinous flocks and herds, which must have been spread out over a district as large as a good-sized English county. . . . And what of the sick and infirm, or the women in recent and imminent childbirth, in a population like that of LONDON, where the births are 264 a-day, or about one in every five minutes? But this is a very small part of the difficulty. We are required to believe that, in one single day, the order to start was communicated suddenly, at midnight, to every single family of every town and village; that in obedience to such order having first 'borrowed' very largely from their Egyptian neighbours in all directions, they then came in from all parts of the land of Goshen to Rameses, bringing with them the sick and infirm, the young and the aged; further, that since receiving the summons, they had sent out to gather in all their flocks and herds, spread over so wide a district, and had driven them also to Rameses; and lastly, that having done all this since they were

roused at midnight, they were started again from Rameses to Succoth, not leaving a single sick or infirm person, a single woman in childbirth, or even a 'single hoof' (Ex. x. 26) behind them."

Having thus stated his case, the Bishop proceeds to narrate a personal incident, of having, with his household, been roused from bed by a false alarm, and he says: " Remembering, as I do, the confusion in my own small household of thirty or forty persons, I do not hesitate to declare this statement to be utterly incredible and impossible." While we may express our cordial sympathy with the Bishop and his suffering household upon *their* sorrowful march at midnight, there can be no lack of feeling in pointing out that there is not the slightest analogy between the cases, and that such a reminiscence is entirely out of place in a Critical Examination, tending only to enlist the sympathy of the reader at the expense of his judgment. Thus, the Bishop's family were slumbering; every Jew was up and dressed. The Bishop and his household were *at home;* the Jews were in the country of their enemies and oppressors, and were quite ready and willing to depart. The Bishop's family apparently knew not where to go for shelter; the Jews had a military organization and a leader, who held frequent communion with Jehovah. Many other differences might be pointed out, but these will suffice. There is, however, another remark which appears to be called for. When the Bishop is natural, and not critical, he speaks quietly of his own *small* household of thirty or forty persons. The most he will allow for a Jewish household in Egypt is fifteen, but surely we may suppose that a household in a crowded Egyptian Treasure City was as large as one in the wilds of South Africa, without incurring any imputation of extravagance in our supposition.

In order to do justice to the subject under discussion, we shall divide the Bishop's statements into different assertions, as in the previous chapter, using in all cases the Bishop's own words:—

Assertion 1. "We are required to believe that in one single day the order to start was communicated suddenly, at midnight, to every single family."

Assertion 2. "The people to whom this order was to be given must have occupied a tract of land as large as Hertfordshire, but ten times as thickly peopled."

Assertion 3. "They occupied part of the night in 'borrowing' from the Egyptians."

Assertion 4. "They then came in from all parts of the land of Goshen to Rameses."

Assertion 5. "They brought with them all the sick and the infirm."

Assertion 6. "Since receiving the summons, they had sent out to gather in all their flocks and herds, and had driven them also to Rameses."

Assertion 7. "Having done all this since they were roused at midnight, they were started again from Rameses that very same day, and marched on to Succoth, not leaving a single sick or infirm person, a single woman in childbirth, or even a single hoof behind them."

"This is undoubtedly what the story in Exodus requires us to believe," asserts the Bishop. Before accepting the necessity, and arguing from the Bishop's assertions, we will carefully examine his representations, and ascertain how far they are warranted by a perusal of the narrative.

Assertion 1. "We are required to believe that the order to start was communicated suddenly, at midnight, to every single family."

To this we answer, the order and time of starting had been arranged, they knew they were going, they had prepared everything in readiness to start, they were warned beforehand that they should be thrust out, and they were thrust out, by the stricken and maddened Egyptians.

Assertion 2. " The people to whom this order was given must have occupied a tract of land as large as Hertfordshire, but ten times as thickly peopled."

When it suits the Bishop's purpose, he can quote passages from Josephus. As it suits ours now in demurring to this assertion, we shall follow his example, and offer the following for the Bishop's consideration in solving this objection :—" Accordingly he (Moses) having got the Hebrews ready for their departure, and having sorted the people into tribes, *he kept them together in one place.*" *De Bell. Jud.*, book ii., chap. xiv. 6.

We do not know the Bishop's authority for this assertion, there is none given in his book. We have no statistical information concerning the district they occupied, but certainly the warned people would gather as closely together as possible in readiness to depart, and not only the Hebrews, but the Egyptians also, must have known that the death of the first-born was connected with the departure of the Israelites, or why should they connect such dissimilar things? What but a revelation and knowledge of the true cause of their sorrow should cause the masters to thrust out their slaves, as the narrative informs us they did?

Assertion 3. " They occupied part of the night in ' borrowing' from the Egyptians."

This assertion is simply a repetition of what the Bishop evidently considers a strong objection, and as we have shown in the previous chapter that it is utterly opposed to the plain statement in the narrative in Exodus, we need not waste time in repeating our refutation.

Assertion 4. " They came in from all parts of the land of Goshen to Rameses."

Will the Bishop kindly inform us what distance in miles, or furlongs, or even yards, they had to travel to accomplish this wonderful feat, for surely a Bishop of the Church of England, thinking himself competent to enter upon a Critical Examination, should be able easily to answer the question. To enable him to do so we will ask him to read the following Scriptures :—" Pharaoh spake unto Joseph, saying, Thy father and thy brethren are come unto thee, the land of Egypt is before thee, in the best of the land make thy father and brethren to dwell, in the land of Goshen let them dwell," Gen. xlvii. 6; compared with ver. 11 in the same chapter, " And Joseph placed his father and his brethren, and gave them a possession in the land of Egypt, in the best of the land, in the land of Rameses, as Pharaoh had commanded." So Goshen and Rameses were identical, and they went out from the same place where Joseph had installed them 215 years before.

רעמסס, Rameses, is either the land of Goshen, or the district in which Goshen is laid. It must not be confounded with the towns bearing the same name, which the Israelites either built or fortified, Ex. i. 11, for, as Aben Ezra points out, the city is רַעַמְסֵס, Raamses, whereas the land is רַעְמְסֵס Raameses. According to Yablonsky, this name is composed of the Cophtic words, *Rem* (romi) man, and *Schos*, shepherd. The name Rem-Schos, Ramses would, therefore, like the Greek Βουκολιά, signify the land of *Sheep-herdsmen*, and would then appear as perfectly identical with Goshen. This derivation is still further confirmed by I. Rossi, who derives ΣΧΩC, *Shepherd*, from ΣΧΩCX, shame, or disgrace. The Septuagint, who wrote Ραμεσσῆ, always considered the land of Raamses as identical with Goshen. All other ancient versions, except Jonathan, and the Arabic version of R. Saadias Gaon, retain the name Raamses when speaking of Goshen.

Assertion 5. " They brought with them the sick and the infirm," so says the Bishop.

" There was not one feeble person among their tribes," so says the Bible, Psalm, cv. 37.

Assertion 6. " Since receiving the summons they had sent out to gather in all their flocks and herds, and had driven them also to Rameses."

This is a perfectly disgraceful example of manufacturing a difficulty, for which the very best excuse that we can possibly make is, that it is founded on the ignorance of the objector. We have shown clearly, in answer to Assertion 5, that Rameses and Goshen were identical, and yet here the Bishop calls upon us to allow time for gathering and driving the sheep and cattle from one place to another. It need hardly be said that there is no warrant for this statement in Exodus. It may be characterised as an invention coolly put forward as truth, in order to bolster up a hopelessly bad case, a very saddening specimen of a "made" fact.

Assertion 7. "Having done all this since they were roused at midnight, they were started again from Rameses that very same day, and marched on to Succoth, not leaving a single sick or infirm person, a single woman in childbirth, or even a single hoof behind them."

Having done all this, driven their cattle from Goshen to Rameses, two names for one place; they were *not* roused at midnight; we have shown they were watching and waiting, and there were no sick or infirm persons to care for, Ps. cv. 37. Nor can it be shown that even women in childbirth would be such hindrances as to detract at all from the probability of this Exodus when we remember the little pain or trouble some women experience during parturition. That this was pre-eminently the case amongst the Hebrews, is shown in the Narrative, and a very late traveller has asserted, "that the women in the fields at work are accustomed to go behind a hedge, deliver themselves, and resume their labour." There is also no reason whatever to suppose that the women in such a case had to perform the journey by walking. They came down into Egypt 215 years before in wagons, which had been expressly sent for them, Gen. xlv. 19 : there were at least three different kinds of chariots in common use in Egypt at this time and long before, *i. e.*, the chariot of state, the war chariots, and the transport wagons for goods. This being the case, it is perfectly natural to suppose that a sufficient number of conveyances for any women who might be in childbirth, and for the young children, would be willingly provided by the Egyptians, in their anxiety to get rid of the Israelites, and there is even a hint of some conveyance in the narrative itself, where it states, "the children of Israel journeyed from Rameses to Succoth, about six hundred thousand *on foot* that were men, beside children," Ex. xii. 37 ; and if the able-bodied thus marched on foot, while conveyance was provided for the women in childbirth, and the little children, there is not the slightest difficulty in believing that the travellers accomplished the different journeys as they are stated in the narrative.

" And now," says the Bishop, " let us see them on the march itself. If we imagine the people to have travelled through the open desert in a wide body, fifty men abreast, as some suppose to have been the practice in the Hebrew armies, then allowing an interval of a yard between each rank, the able-bodied warriors alone would have filled up the road for about *seven miles*, and the whole multitude would have formed a dense column more than *twenty-two miles* long."

The Bishop here says we may imagine one long line of twenty-two miles; we prefer to imagine something more business-like and real, founded on knowledge of the statement of the circumstances put forth in the narrative, and what little is known of contemporary history. Caravans on a large scale, to and from Egypt, could not have been unknown to Moses, who was formerly a prince of that land, nor could he have been ignorant of their management. (See Calmet, Frag. 1). We may here also remember the assertion of Josephus, that Moses had previously sorted the people into tribes; and consequently very reasonably imagine that from the land of Goshen or Rameses, divided into as many parties, starting from as many centres, by as many roads as seemed right to their skilful and heaven-directed leader, the people, high in heart and hope, went up from bondage. We may reasonably imagine the Egyptians giving every possible assistance, sedulously supplying every want, in order to rid themselves of their former slaves with greater speed, and in their sorrow and fear bowing abjectly before Moses, begging him with heartfelt entreaty to depart at once; employing themselves in any and every way that could expedite the object in view, so much so as to justify the remark of a friend of ours, that without doubt there were two Egyptians ready and willing to carry the luggage of every single Jew, to help him drive flocks and herds, assist the women and children, and in short, do all that was in their power to get them out of the land; until the very latest straggler had departed towards the common rendezvous at Succoth. Where that may have been, whether it was a city, a station in the desert, or simply the booths of the cattle on the edge of the wilderness, we are not informed. Upon the minutiæ of this journey; what the Israelites and their cattle had to eat and to drink, the narrative is perfectly silent. It is allowable to suggest that it might have been wiser in the Bishop if he had followed the reticent example.

"CHAPTER XII.

"THE SHEEP AND CATTLE OF THE ISRAELITES IN THE DESERT." Quotation :—"*And the children of Israel did eat manna for forty years, until they came to a land inhabited; they did eat manna until they came unto the borders of the land of Canaan.*"—Ex. xvi. 35.

This is the Bishop's statement: "The *people*, we are told, were supplied with manna. But there was no miraculous provision of food for the herds and flocks. They were left to gather sustenance as they could in that inhospitable wilderness. We will now go on to consider the possibility of such a multitude of cattle finding any means of support, for forty years, under these circumstances. And first it is certain that the story represents them as *possessing* these flocks and herds during the whole of the forty years which they spent in the wilderness. Thus in the *second* year, Moses asks, 'Shall the flocks and the herds be slain for them to suffice them?' Num. xi. 22. And in the fortieth year we read, 'The children of Reuben and the children of Gad had a very great multitude of cattle,' Num. xxxii. 1. We find that, at the end of the *first* year, they kept the second Passover under Sinai, Num. ix. 5, and therefore, we may presume, had at that time, as before, 200,000 male lambs of the first year at their command, and two millions of sheep and oxen close at hand."

Bishop Colenso quotes passages from Canon Stanley's "Sinai and Palestine," passages which no one will be inclined to dispute, showing the present sterility of the desert through which the Israelites passed on their journey, and in which they spent nearly forty years. Then he assumes from the fact of present sterility that the desert was in the time of the Israelites in the same condition, and joining the facts of sterility and the numerous flocks of the Israelites, he declares that the two halves produce a whole which is incredible. The Bishop's objections being divided into two parts: the lack of green food for the cattle, and of water for man and beast.

Let us consider the lack of water first. To support his assertion, the Bishop quotes Num. xx. 4, 5, "'Why have ye brought up the congregation of Jehovah into this wilderness, that we and our cattle should die there? Wherefore have ye made us to come up out of Egypt, to bring us unto this evil place? It is no place of seed, or of figs, or of vines, or of pomegranates, neither is there any water to drink.' From this passage it appears also that the water from the rock did *not* follow them, as some have supposed." There is no doubt that the Bishop in this last assertion trusted to a misty remembrance that some one had asserted the water from the rock did follow them, and as it did not suit his purpose to admit that assertion, he thus puts it on one side. But as the assertion happens to be made by a man before whose human learning even, that of the Bishop of Natal is less than nothing, not to speak of his inspiration, we shall here place his testimony in opposition to that of Dr. Colenso. It is Paul who says, "They did all drink of that spiritual rock that followed (marg., went with) them, and that rock was Christ." Here the apostle of the living God distinctly asserts the very position which the Bishop denies; and as we have not a shadow of doubt which it is most reasonable to believe, we shall leave the controversy there.

But we will examine the passages quoted by the Bishop a little more closely. The Israelites are murmuring, and declaring their wants, and no man in his senses will doubt they made the case as bad as it was possible to make it. And what are their requirements? Luxuries for themselves, and water for selves and cattle; seed, figs, vines, pomegranates, for themselves, and water for themselves and the cattle. Not a word or a hint about lack of fodder for the cattle. And when the water was miraculously given, even then not a hint of scarcity of food for flock or herd.

The Bishop quotes the Israelitish complaint of that great and terrible wilderness wherein were fiery serpents, scorpions, and drought, but not a word of complaint respecting hungry cattle, starving sheep, fainting and famished flock and herd, surely this would have been mentioned had the scarcity existed. Again, complaints of the wilderness, of deserts, and of pits, but not a word of the awful scourge of hungry cattle. On the supposition of the truth of the narrative, we must therefore assume that there was sufficient food for the cattle; on the supposition of its falsehood, we arrive at the following highly original and satisfactory conclusion,—that the narrator knew that cattle might be thirsty, but was ignorant that they ever wanted any thing to eat; for to assume that the chronicler was ignorant of the characteristics of the desert he has so minutely pictured, is simply ridiculous. Even the Bishop himself assumes, and strives hard to prove (which is a perfectly needless task) that the vivid picture of the desert in the narrative is truthful in its every detail. It must not be forgotten that the cattle are mentioned repeatedly; that when the lack of water occurs, that lack is loudly proclaimed; but throughout the narrative there is not one hint that even scarcity of food was during all the forty years experienced by flock or herd.

There are some other considerations which must here be mentioned; the first is—That at least *some* parts of the desert were fitted to sustain cattle; this is shown in Ex. iii. 1, "Now Moses kept the flock of Jethro, his father-in-law, the priest of Midian, and he led the flock to the back side of the desert, and came to the mountain of God, even to Horeb." It is plain from this passage that Moses, having a choice of pasturages, led his flocks into one of the very places where, the Bishop declares, there was nothing for them to eat. The second consideration is, That large and fertile oases may have existed at the period of the narrative which have since become like the rest of the desert. That this is not impossible is shown by the present desert condition of large portions of Palestine itself, where whole tracts of land which once supported large numbers in luxury, are now pictures of sterility and barrenness; and the Bishop himself points out an agency by which this could easily have been accomplished when he alludes to the frequent sand-storms, by which that region is characterized. The third consideration is, that as the Israelites themselves were supported by miraculous provision, their sheep and cattle may have been cared for in the same manner; but we have no right to assume such a miracle, and therefore lay no stress upon the old Jewish tradition that this really was the case; but if we have no right to assume a miracle, the Bishop has no right to assume the negation of all means of support for cattle that are frequently mentioned, and therefore constantly in the mind of the narrator. The last consideration is, the frequent removal of the camp of the Israelites might be occasioned by this necessity of the food for the cattle; there were above forty different encampments during the stay in the desert, and while this assumption supplies a probable and natural reason for change, we are not aware that any other has ever been given. The agency for the direction of removals, the pillar of cloud and fire, is well known, but the necessity for removals is not mentioned.

It should also be remembered that the complaints of the Israelites were comparative, they went from one land of absolute profusion to another of still greater abundance, and this very fact of remembered plenty with clearly promised profusion would render the intermediate barrenness still more apparent, and hard to bear. In concluding this subject, we would observe that the immense number of the flocks and herds is simply assumed by the Bishop; there is no foundation whatever for believing that 200,000 lambs were ever required for the Passover in Egypt or in the Wilderness, *and it is upon this groundwork of imagination alone that all the Bishop's suppositions upon this subject are reared.* That the flocks and herds were there, and that they were fed, is negatively proved by the prohibition the Bishop has quoted: "Neither let the flocks nor herds feed before that mount," Ex. xxxiv. 3. If there were no flocks there, nor anything for them to eat, the prohibition is simply ridiculous; and with all his striving, the Bishop has not yet succeeded in casting ridicule upon the Pentateuch, and it needs no gift of prophecy to foresee he never will.

"CHAPTER XIII.

"THE NUMBER OF THE ISRAELITES COMPARED WITH THE EXTENT OF THE LAND OF CANAAN." Quotation:—"*I will send my fear before thee, and will destroy all the people to whom thou shalt come, and I will make all thine enemies turn their backs unto thee. And I will send hornets before thee, which shall drive out the Hivite, the Canaanite, and the Hittite, from before thee. I will not drive them out from before thee in one year, lest the land become desolate, and the beast of the field multiply against thee. By little and little I will drive them out from before thee, until thou be increased and inherit the land.*"—Ex. xxiii. 27—30.

The Bishop's objection here is, that the danger spoken of in the 29th verse—the land becoming desolate, and the beast of the field multiplying against the people—could not possibly exist. He states that the land to be divided among the tribes in the time of Joshua was about 7,000,000 acres, while Bagster's Comprehensive Bible gives more than double that quantity, 14,976,000 acres, as the area of the land of Canaan. He instances the population and extent of the English counties of Norfolk, Suffolk, and Essex, as a case in point, and his argument is, that there could be no more danger of desolation or overrunning in one case than in the other. We venture to characterize the comparison as inaccurate and unfair, if it be not especially designed to mislead. To hold good, it must be shown that there is no more danger of desolation and overrunning in unsettled times and places than in settled; that the desolation well known to be produced by war in the countries afflicted with that curse is simply a myth; that even a war of conquest amounting to extermination would have no effect upon the agricultural condition of a country. The Bishop's supposition carries with it the exceedingly improbable assumption of the old inhabitants keeping the land in "high heart," as it is termed, and handing it over in splendid condition to the new occupants, who slew them by way of recompense. Of course the Narrative is in no way responsible for such absurd suppositions, nor does it anywhere state that this desolation or overrunning really occurred; the prevention that was adopted succeeded to perfection, and the whole passage quoted by the Bishop is a beautiful illustration of the minute care of Jehovah for his chosen people, and corroboration of another passage, Deut. xxxii. 10—12: "He found him in a desert land, and in the waste howling wilderness; He led him about, He instructed him, He kept him as the apple of his eye. As an eagle stirreth up her nest, fluttereth over her young, spreadeth abroad her wings, taketh them, beareth them on her wings; so the Lord alone did lead him, and there was no strange God with him."

"CHAPTER XIV.

"The Number of the First-born compared with the Number of Male Adults." Quotation :—"*All the first-born males, from a month old and upward, of those that were numbered, were twenty and two thousand two hundred and three score and thirteen.*"—Num. iii. 43.

The Bishop states his objection as follows :—" Let us see what this statement implies when treated as a simple matter of fact. For this purpose I quote the words of Kurtz (iii. 209). If there were 600,000 males of twenty years and upwards, the whole number of males may be reckoned at 900,000 (he elsewhere reckons

1,000 000), in which case there would be only one first-born to 42 (44) males. In other words, the number of boys in every family must have been, on the average, forty-two. This will be seen at once if we consider that the rest of the 900,000 males were *not* first-borns; and, therefore, each of these must have had one or the other of the 22,273 as the first-born of his own family, except, of course, in any case where the first-born of any family was a daughter or was dead."

That the Bishop of Natal considers this a very strong, if not perfectly insoluble objection, is proved by some remarks made at the end of this chapter, which will be quoted and commented on in their proper place. We must, therefore, proceed cautiously in our endeavour to discover and show the real weight and character of the objection; and for this purpose we shall seek out and state the Bishop's assertions in his own words:—

Assertion 1. " According to the story of the Pentateuch every mother of Israel must have had forty-two sons."

Assertion 2. "We have no reason whatever to suppose from the data which we find in the Pentateuch, that the mothers of Israel were prolific in any unusual degree."

Assertion 3. "It is a pure assumption, and unwarranted by anything that is found in Scripture, that such of the first-born as were themselves heads of families, were not reckoned at all as first-born."

Assertion 4. "The number of *mothers* must have been the same as that of the first-born, male and female; hence there would have been only 60,000 women to 600,000 men, so that only one man in ten had a wife or children."

So asserts the Bishop. It is evident that there is a gross and ridiculous error somewhere; we shall now endeavour to discover where this error lies.

Upon the Bishop's showing, Kurtz, Michaelis, Havernick, and

Bunsen, take the statement as it stands for granted, and endeavour to explain it; but Scott appears to us to give an outline of a true and satisfactory solution which we shall endeavour to fill up and enlarge upon. To do this, we will first look closely into the passages concerned, in order to ascertain step by step the intent and extent of the commandment concerning the first-born.

The Israelites had been released from slavery; and from all external dictation they were as free as the air of the wilderness in which they were sojourning. In order to their enjoyment of complete freedom combined with the advantages of civilization, long, laborious, and incessant training was absolutely necessary. A form of government was instituted—that form was Theocratic, and there can be no Theocracy without worship; for convenience of worship, one central sanctuary was decreed, and a very minute, intricate, and laborious series of services were commanded to be established; to perform these services a large number of *able-bodied men* were required; and the manner in which these were supplied forms the true and proper groundwork of the inquiry now before us.

At the time of the Exodus from Egypt the commandment is given to Moses in the words following, Ex. xiii. 2: "Whatsoever openeth the womb.... of man and of beast, it (is) mine." It is to be noticed that this is simply the preliminary announcement to Moses; not stated at that time to be even made known to the children of Israel generally. When the commandments and the law were given at Sinai, the subject is again mentioned with the plain direction that the commandment should only apply to those born subsequently. We shall quote this direction as it completely destroys the theory on which the Bishop's objection is founded, and destroys it so completely that it is difficult to conceive he had ever read the passage: "The first-born of thy sons shalt thou give unto Me; likewise shalt thou do with thine oxen and with thy sheep: seven days it shall be with his dam; *on the eighth day thou shalt give it Me,*" Ex. xxii. 29, 30. It is evident that this passage could only apply to the first-born of man and beast thereafter to be born, for if the commandment had a retrospective effect, this last direction concerning the eighth day would have rendered obedience out of the question, a retrospective law *must* have stultified itself. The next mention of the law provides for the redemption of the first-born by money or substitution, Ex. xxxiv. 20; the following enactment provides against any man sanctifying that which is already sanctified, Lev. xxvii. 26, 27; and then follows the setting apart and numbering of the first-born, Num. iii. 40; and the number of individuals thus obtained, we are told in the verse quoted by the Bishop was 22,273; but these being only children of from one to thirteen months old at the utmost (*i.e.*, born between the Exodus and the completion of the Tabernacle), would have been utterly useless for the very purpose for which they were separated. They could not have accomplished the work of the sanctuary, and therefore the families of the tribe of Levi are taken in the place of the first-born, and by them all the service of the sanctuary is performed.

Looking thus at the subject as a whole, gathered from the narrative, it is perfectly inconceivable how the Bishop could have fallen into the foolish error he has magnified into a formidable objection. Indeed it requires a large amount of charity to believe that the misrepresentation here is not wilful, inasmuch as there is so clear an intimation of reservation in the text on which the Bishop founds his objection, that it cannot be passed over if read with ordinary attention, and certainly indicates the necessity of further research. The Bishop quotes Num. iii. 43, "all the first-born males, from a month old and upward, *of those that were numbered;*" and if this reservation has any meaning at all, it implies that there were first-born, who, for some reason not there stated, were not included in the census, and in the 13th verse (precedent to that quoted by the Bishop from the narrative) we are distinctly told the reason of the reservation: "All the first-born are mine; for on the day that I smote all the first-born of the land of Egypt, I hallowed unto me all the first-born in Israel, both man and beast."

To sum up this somewhat lengthy statement in a few words:
—The Lord sanctified all the first-born of Israel, man and beast, from the day of the Exodus. In about one year the first-born male children numbered 22,273, and the families of the tribe of Levi were taken in their stead.

We will now contrast this clear and consistent statement of the Narrative respecting the first-born, with the assertions of the Bishop, and ascertain the answers that are therein given:—

Assertion 1. "According to the story of the Pentateuch, every mother in Israel must have had forty-two sons."

This assertion is founded on the assumption that all the first-born, of what age soever, were included in the census, which cannot be shown. It assumes, in fact, that there was only as many mothers in all Israel as first-born male children in one year, or thirteen months at the farthest.

Assertion 2. "We have no reason whatever to suppose from the data which we find in the Pentateuch, that the mothers of Israel were prolific in any unusual degree."

It is not at all necessary to our present argument to prove that they were; but the fact is directly contrary to the statement of the Bishop: for, if from the numerical data—*i.e.*, from the number of children named and specified—this assertion may possibly be regarded as true, the Bible contains other data beside numbers; and in contrast with the Bishop's assertion we simply place the following passages: "And Israel dwelt in the land of Egypt, in the country of Goshen; and they had possessions therein, and grew, and *multiplied exceedingly*," Gen. xlvii. 27. "And the children of Israel were fruitful, and increased abundantly, and waxed exceeding mighty, and *the land was filled with them*," Ex. i. 7. "The more they afflicted them, *the more they multiplied and grew*," Ex. i. 12.

Assertion 3. " It is pure assumption, and unwarranted by anything that is found in Scripture, that such of the first-born as were themselves heads of families were not reckoned at all as first-born."

The assumption in this assertion is, that first-born heads of families having offspring, were to be reckoned among the first-born and redeemed; but unless it can be shown that a different law applied to man and beast, which nowhere appears, the assertion is at once seen to be absurd when applied to the cattle and sheep, the direction being that they were to be killed on the eighth day; therefore, the supposition of the Bishop as to retrospective action of the law is simply an absurdity.

Assertion 4. "The number of the mothers must have been the same as that of the first-born, male and female, and dead—so that allowing 60,000 mothers, only one man in ten had a wife or children."

There can be no question as to the number of mothers being identical with that of the first-born; but the gross total of the number of the first-born is nowhere stated or even hinted at, and consequently there is not the slightest data from which to ascertain the number of mothers. Any question about their number is idle, and can only tend to distract from the true issue, or to prejudice the minds of the readers of the Bishop's book.

But, objects the Bishop to this solution of his pet difficulty, it is stated *all* the first-born were to be taken. This *all* is, of course, subject to the provisions of the law itself, and that it could not possibly apply as the Bishop would have us believe, is clearly shown in the direction concerning the cattle on the eighth day; it is indisputable that if the law were retrospective, it could not be obeyed.

Thus, the whole of the Bishop's carefully-reared "card castle" falls to the ground; his elaborate calculations, his foolish idea of 60,000 wives amongst 600,000 men, his sapient imagining of 42 children in every family, is shown to be simply unnecessary and ridiculous. The gross number of the first-born in Israel being unknown, any argument raised upon mere supposition is unworthy of notice beyond pointing out the fallacy upon which it is erected.

But upon this foundation of elaborate folly, the Bishop rears a superstructure of awful wickedness, for here for the first time he claims his reader for a brother infidel. On the faith of this nonsensical calculation he proceeds to assume that we must give up our belief in the historical truth of the Pentateuch. We write awful wickedness, and we write as we think and feel, that it is awful wickedness for one in high station, living by the gospel, himself a recipient of the shekel hakkodesh, to ask ignorant and unlearned men to follow him into infidelity, on the faith of a few objections unfairly stated in every case; with the vast mass of affirmative evidence utterly ignored; asked to become infidels on the *ex parte* statements of a mere unscrupulous advocate, and that advocacy itself the blackest treason to the cause he had solemnly sworn to defend. We make these remarks because here the Bishop stops his criticism for a time and thus writes:—" By this time surely great doubt must have arisen in the mind of most readers as to the historical veracity of sundry portions of the Pentateuch." And this is our reply to the insinuated question—" Bishop of the Church of England, we, two working men, having *carefully read and pondered every sentence you have written* up to this point, answer you emphatically, and with all our souls, No; but that an exactly contrary effect has been produced upon our minds, by the very small amount of study of God's Truth (God's Truth, a thousand times, Bishop) necessary to answer *you* hitherto. We are more thoroughly convinced than ever, that every word of God is true; that all Scripture, historical and otherwise, is given by inspiration of God, and that any man of average capacity, though he never saw anything else but an English Bible, with the references in the margin, may, by an attentive study and comparison of one passage of Scripture with others, dissolve all your objections, by proving that they are utterly destitute of foundation in the narrative from which they are falsely professed to have been taken.

When you are lying upon your deathbed, and your spent life is passing in rapid review before you, it may be some small satisfaction to you to know that at least two of the class to whom your book is calculated to be most dangerous, after careful examination, are convinced of its utter groundlessness and folly. Alas for you! that so many of our brethren of the working classes will accept your conclusions, never troubling themselves with any inquiry as to the mode by which you have arrived at them. Alas for you and them! that your book was offered and accepted as a fitting and sufficient substitute, in an Infidel Hall on the Evening of the holy Sabbath, for the blasphemous rant of their most unscrupulous advocate. "It must needs be that offences come, but woe to that man by whom the offence cometh," Matt. xviii. 7. We will only add, in reference to your appeal, that there is one subject on which your book has left no shadow of a doubt on our minds, and that is as to your own personal fitness to occupy the position and do the work you have undertaken, as a faithful minister of the Church of England.

"CHAPTERS XV., XVI., XVII.

"THE SOJOURNING OF THE ISRAELITES. THE EXODUS IN THE FOURTH GENERATION. THE NUMBER OF ISRAELITES AT THE TIME OF THE EXODUS."—There is but one quotation to these three chapters—"*Now the sojourning of the children of Israel, who dwelt in Egypt, was four hundred and thirty years,*" Ex. xii. 40,—and as the first and second are simply introductory to the third, it will be more convenient to regard these chapters as a complete subject. The Bishop thus remarks:—"It is plain that the 430 years are meant, as St. Paul understood, to be reckoned from the time of the call of Abraham; thus, reckoning 25 years from his leaving Haran to the birth of Isaac, 60 years to the birth of Jacob, 130 years to the migration into Egypt, we have 215 years' sojourning in the land of Canaan, leaving just the same length of time, 215 years, for the sojourn in the land of Egypt. We must conclude, then, that the translation in the English Bible of Ex. xii. 40, however awkwardly it reads, is correct as it stands, *if the Hebrew words themselves are correct*, as they appear in all manuscript and printed copies of the Pentateuch.

"Again, when it is said, Gen. xv. 16, 'In the *fourth* generation they shall come hither again;' this can only mean in the *fourth* generation, reckoning from the time when they should leave the land of Canaan, and go down into Egypt. Thus we find Moses and Aaron in the fourth generation from the time of the migration, viz., Jacob, Levi, Kohath, Amram, Aaron; or, as Jacob was so aged, and Moses and Aaron also were advanced in life beyond the military age, we may reckon from those, as Levi, who went down into Egypt in the prime of life, and then the generation of Joshua, Eleazar, etc., in the prime of life, will be the fourth generation. We conclude, then, that it is an indisputable fact, that the story as it is told in the Pentateuch intends it to be understood—1. That the children of Israel came out of Egypt about 215 years after they went down thither, in the time of Jacob. 2. That they came out in the fourth generation from the adults in the prime of life who went down with Jacob, and it should be observed that the second of these conclusions does not in any way depend upon the former. From this it can be shown, beyond a doubt, that it is quite impossible that there should have been such a number of the people of Israel in Egypt, at the time of the Exodus, as to have furnished 600,000 warriors in the prime of life, representing at least two millions of persons of all ages and sexes, that is to say, it is impossible *if we will take the data, to be derived from the Pentateuch itself.*"

We have thus summarized the arguments and statements of the Bishop which are contained in his Chapters xv. and xvi., the whole of which lead up to the statement which the Bishop thus makes :—" It is quite impossible that there should have been such a number of the people of Israel in Egypt at the time of the Exodus, as to have furnished 600,000 warriors in the prime of life, representing at least two millions of persons."

Now as the Bible distinctly and unmistakably declares that such was the fact, the Bishop and the Bible are at plain issue ; for the Bible states plainly there were 600,000 men in the prime of life, and the Bishop rejoins, " Quite impossible."

This being the plain and clear question raised, we shall first consider what the Bishop has to say to prove the case he has brought forward, and then ascertain what reply can be given from a plain common-sense study of God's Holy Word.

The assertions of the Bishop are as follows :—

Assertion 1. "We nowhere read of any very large families among the children of Jacob, or their descendants, to the time of the Exodus."

Assertion 2. "The wonderful preponderance of males in the

family of Jacob is another indication of the unhistorical character of the whole account."

Assertion 3. "The twelve sons of Jacob had between them 53 sons, average four and a-half each."

Assertion 4. "If the number of *all* the males in the four generations be added together, they would only amount to 6611. If we even add to these the number of the fifth generation, 22,154, who would be mostly children, the sum total of males of all generations could not, according to their data, have exceeded 28,465, instead of being 1,000,000."

We may fairly take the above as the Bishop's assertions on this large subject, and we now proceed to see how far they agree with the Scripture narrative.

Assertion 1. "We *nowhere* read of any very large families among the children of Jacob or their descendants, to the time of the Exodus."

We shall simply compare the following Scriptures (some of which have been before quoted) with the Bishop's remarkably cool assertion. "And Israel dwelt in the land of Egypt, in the country of Goshen; and they had possessions therein, *and grew, and multiplied exceedingly*," Gen. xlvii. 27. " The children of Israel were fruitful, and increased abundantly, and multiplied, and waxed exceeding mighty; and *the land was filled with them*," Ex. i. 7. "The more they afflicted them, the more they multiplied and grew," Ex. i. 12. " Thy fathers went down into Egypt with threescore and ten persons; and now the Lord thy God hath made thee as the stars of heaven for multitude," Deut. x. 22. "A Syrian ready to perish was my father; and he went down into Egypt, and sojourned there with a few, and became there a nation, great, mighty, and populous," Deut. xxvi. 5. It will be seen that these texts constitute a direct contradiction to the first assertion of the Bishop, and any comment is superfluous.

Assertion 2. "The wonderful preponderance of males in Jacob's family is another indication of the unhistorical character of the whole account."

This objection is so exceedingly trivial that it is scarcely worthy of notice, for when analyzed it amounts to neither more nor less than this—The Bishop's objection to the narrative is, that it asserts that one woman had six sons and a daughter, and three other women had two sons each; that is to say, that any document that asserts that a woman had six sons and one daughter cannot be true. To show the fallacy of the Bishop's argument it is sufficient to state, that one of our fellow-workmen has by *one* wife a family of nine sons and one daughter. Would the Bishop venture to tell our fellow-workman that the register in his Family Bible is "historically untrue?" We think it right to add that this paragraph of the Bishop's book was read in our shop and received with a shout of derisive laughter.

Assertion 3. "The twelve sons of Jacob had between them fifty-three sons, average four and a-half each."

It appears to us that in this assertion lies the fallacy of all the figures the Bishop has so industriously gathered on this subject, and this we hope very clearly to show. The Bishop tells us in the course of the foregoing chapters that Judah was 42 years of age when he went down to Egypt (we think he was a few years older); Joseph was then 39, and Benjamin younger, so that at the time of the descent into Egypt, Reuben would be certainly under 50, and Benjamin a little more than 40, at the utmost. Now, Abraham had a son when he was 100 years old; Isaac was 60 when Esau and Jacob were born, and Jacob must have been more than 80 before the birth of his eldest son; and yet *the Bishop's assumption upon which all his arguments and figures are based* is, that these twelve sons of Jacob, though in the full strength and prime of manhood, *had no more sons born to them after they went down into Egypt;* that is, that Levi lived 57 years in Egypt without having a child, then had one daughter born to him, but no sons, during 70 or 80 years; that no one among his eleven brethren had any more sons; that Benjamin had ten sons before he was forty years of age, but none afterwards; that Joseph had two sons within seven years, but no more during 70 years of after life; that Jacob himself had twelve sons after he was 80 years old, but none of his sons had offspring after 50, with one exception, and some of them, not after half the age of their father at the birth of his eldest son; that the wives of Jacob's sons, up to this time, had been exceedingly fruitful, but after they went into Egypt they suddenly and unaccountably ceased to bear children. All these anomalies, and many more, we must believe, in order to endorse the Bishop's *assumption.*

On the positive side of this question there are the following *facts.* We are expressly told in Genesis that Joseph had other sons; these are the words (chap. xlviii. 5, 6), Jacob speaks:—
"Thy two sons, Ephraim and Manasseh, which were born unto thee in the land of Egypt, before I came unto thee into Egypt are mine; as Reuben and Simeon, they shall be mine. And thy issue which thou begettest [Heb. *which thou hast begotten*] after them shall be thine, and shall be called by the name of their brethren after them in their inheritance." After Jacob's death, the youngest of his grandchildren that came *with him* into Egypt must have been more than seventeen years of age. Joseph's brethren came to him fearing he would remember and revenge former injuries, and they gave him a touching message from lips then silent for ever; from their father, whose darling Joseph had been. They said (Gen. l. 17, 21), Our father said before he died, "Forgive, I pray thee, the trespass of thy brethren and their sin, for they did unto thee evil; and now we pray thee, forgive the trespass of the servants of the God of thy father." And Joseph

replied, "Now, therefore, fear ye not; I will nourish you and your little ones" (Heb. וְאֶת־טַפְּכֶם! little children, *as opposed* to young men and virgins). It will be seen that here is at least an intimation of an indefinite number of children, little children, who were the children of Joseph's brethren, and who must have been born in Egypt, because their parents had been at least seventeen years in Egypt at this time.

But, it is open to the Bishop to object, there are no more names given. This, of course, we admit, and we point to the reason assigned by Jacob himself why no more are given: "Thy issue which thou begettest [Heb., hast begotten] after them, shall be called by the name of their brethren after them in their inheritance." Again, if only those who are mentioned by name are to be counted, then the Bishop's numbers are equally at fault with those, as he asserts, of the Bible. For the Bishop allows there *might* have been 25,000, and it is quite certain that nothing like that number of names appears anywhere in the Narrative. In fact, there is not the shadow of foundation for any numerical data whatever, and the fatal error of the Bishop is very easily pointed out. He has submitted to the test of ordinary averages, a case which as plain as words can state the fact, is expressly removed from their action. He says, average four and a-half sons each; the Bible says, "fruitful exceedingly." He says, in another place, three sons each; the Bible says, "They filled the land." So that the data upon which the calculations are founded are thus proved thoroughly inapplicable; and, consequently, any result arrived at must be idle and worthless.

It appears to us, that by thus pointing out the absence of all reliable data upon which any calculation can be authoritatively founded, the Bishop's objection founded upon his calculations is completely dissolved.

There are, however, other ways of meeting and overcoming

the difficulty; as, in supposing that Jacob brought down many servants with him into Egypt, who are not mentioned by name, but who became incorporated into his family, mixing with, and taking the name of one or the other of the families of Jacob and Joseph's sons, who afterwards became heads of tribes. That such cases of adoption really occurred, we are told in the Narrative (1 Chron. ii. 34, 35), though we have no especial mention of them at the period of the history of which we are now speaking. It is also open to suppose that the sons and grandsons of Jacob themselves took other wives, and had many more children while they dwelt in the land of Egypt, favourites of the king, and cared for and protected by his powerful minister, their own brother; indeed, it must have been a very desirable thing to have been associated with them during the first sixty years of their sojourn in Egypt. The Narrative expressly records that before they were afflicted they multiplied exceedingly, and the more they were afflicted the more they multiplied and grew. It is, therefore, plain that no doctrine of ordinary averages can be applied to such an exceedingly exceptionable case as the one before us.

Assertion 4. "If the number of *all* the males in the four generations be added together, they would only amount to 6311;" with this we must join the assertion that they came out in the fourth generation from the adults in the prime of life.

To answer this assertion we must first ascertain what is meant by a generation in the Hebrew sense of the term, and then which was the fourth of those generations during some period of which the Israelites were again to leave the land of Egypt. Our first question is, What would a Jew understand by the term generation? and his answer would necessarily be determined by the *period of history* to which it was to be applied, inasmuch as the generations of Adam, Jacob, and David were essentially different things, though they are all included in the same general term. Of the time in question, the patriarchal age, the Jew would certainly understand a period of one hundred years, and so says Gesenius ("Heb. and Chal. Lex.," p. 194.): "The Hebrews, like ourselves, appear to have reckoned a generation at from thirty to forty years (see Job xlii. 16), but from the longevity of the patriarchs, in their time it was reckoned at a hundred, Gen. xv. 16, compare v. 14, and Exod. xv. 40." It is worthy of remark, that Gesenius quotes the passage in question to prove that the meaning of the term is one hundred years of time; while the Bishop of Natal uses it to signify the number of men born in about half the same period; so that the foundation upon which the Bishop builds his argument is questionable on a very slight examination.

But to have something like authority to build on, we will take the mean average of Gesenius, and state the generation of men at thirty-five years; thus we shall see it is perfectly possible that there should be six generations of grown men during the 215 years, with five years to spare; nor does it at all follow that all, or nearly all the fourth generation should be dead when the sixth were men grown; for it must not be forgotten, that thousands of the sixth generation might have been thirty years of age; while those of the fourth, their grandfathers, were still of even marriageable age, as Jacob himself was married at certainly nearly eighty years of age, having twelve sons afterward. We shall, therefore, take a generation of men at thirty-five years, adopting the average time stated by Gesenius. We now need another element in the calculation; which is, how many children may fairly be reckoned as constituting a fruitful family. The writer's father had twelve, his brother had ten, himself nine, and is not yet forty years of age; but as we wish to be strictly within the mark, we shall take six healthy children as the result of an exceedingly fruitful marriage; a number to which no reasonable objection can be raised. We shall now take the Bishop's own lowest number as a starting point, 51 grandsons, and we will then see the result, as follows:—

51 grandsons went into Egypt.
6 children each.

306	at the end of 35 years.	
6		
1836	„ 70	„
6		
11,016	„ 105	„
6		
66,096	„ 140	„
6		
396,576	„ 175	„
6		
2,379,456	„ 210	„

We thus see that if we reckon the sixth generation living, with half the fifth, and a quarter of the fourth, there will be 16,000 of the fourth generation living, and more than two and a-half millions in all. Now let us see what all this vast aggregate requires us to believe in individual cases. It is simply this, that in a land of plenty, and among a people especially and exceptionably fruitful, *they married at twenty-one years of age, and had six healthy children each in the following fourteen years.* We have only to give credence to this simple and rational assumption, to be able to believe all that is stated in the narrative, and all that is implied in such statement as set forth by the Bishop himself.

Further, we have only to imagine a number of living grandfathers and grandmothers going up out of Egypt to fulfil every requirement of the narrative, " In the fourth generation they shall come hither again." Nor should it be forgotten that we have the first five years of the seventh generation, to bring into the calculation if still higher numbers were required, but as it is unnecessary, even on the Bishop's own showing, we need do no more than point out the fact. We have also only allowed two generations in seventy years, but it is expressly recorded that Joseph saw Ephraim's *children of the third generation* during that period. So that some of the fourth generation to which the Bishop restricts his calculation, were born within 80 years of the going down into Egypt, and 135 years before the Exodus; that is to say, that there were certainly four generations during the first 100 years, but no more during 135 years afterward; for it must not be forgotten, that the Bishop ends his calculations with Levi's children of the *third* generation, while it is distinctly asserted that his *younger* brother's children of the *fourth* generation were living 135 years before the departure out of Egypt.

We have made these simple and reasonable calculations to show the probability of the numbers in the Narrative being strictly true; but there is not the least foundation in the Narrative upon which such questions of numbers can be satisfactorily based. Any calculation founded upon the mere names given, must be erroneous, inasmuch as they are distinctly stated to be given only in the cases of heads of tribes and families. Names are given only where it was necessary in order to settle questions of descent or genealogy, though there are interspersed here and there notices of celebrities among the children of Israel. It must not be forgotten, that it is nowhere mentioned in the Narrative that complete lists are given; indeed, to have done so, would have defeated the object in view; for *the Pentateuch is a historic sketch, not a census paper.* We will only say by way of summary, that while the Bishop confines himself to four generations, and only grudgingly allows a fifth, the Bible speaks of six, and even seven generations in the lists given in the Chronicles, and there can be no reason to doubt that the statement is correct, when we remember that men commonly lived more than a hundred years, and were certainly in possession of all the powers of manhood for ninety years of that time; or, in other words, that vigorous men of the fourth, and children of the seventh generation went up out of Egypt in company.

"CHAPTER XVIII.

"THE DANITES AND LEVITES AT THE TIME OF THE EXODUS." There is no quotation to this chapter; but the Bishop's objection is as follows: " When we go on further to examine into the details of this large number of male adults the results will be found yet more extravagant. Thus Dan, in the first generation has one son, Gen. xlvi. 23; and that he had no more born to him in the land of Egypt, and therefore had *only* one son appears from Num. xxvi. 42, when the sons of Dan consist of only one family; hence we may reckon that in the fourth generation he would have had 27 warriors descended from him, instead of 62,700 as they are numbered in Num. ii. 26, increased to 64,000 in Num. xxvi. 43. In order to have had this number born to him, we must suppose that Dan's one son and each of *his* sons and grandsons must have had about 80 children of both sexes. We may observe also that the offspring of the *one* son of Dan is represented as nearly double that of the *ten* sons of Benjamin, 35,400, Num. ii. 23. Again we have in Ex. vi. the genealogy before quoted of the three sons of Levi who came with Jacob into Egypt, Gershon, Kohath, Merari; these three increased in the second (Amram's) generation to eight, not to nine as it would have been if they had each three sons on the

THE BIBLE IN THE WORKSHOP. 73

average, viz., the sons of Kohath four, of Gershon two, of Merari two, Ex. vi. 17, 19. The four sons of Kohath increased in the third generation to eight. . . . The two sons of Amram increased in the fourth generation to six, and assuming these proportions to continue, the whole number of Levites who would be numbered at the first census would be only 44, viz., 20 Kohathites 12 Gershonites, 12 Merarites, instead of 8580 as they are numbered in Num. iv. 48, viz., 2750 Kohathites, 2630 Gershonites, 3200 Merarites, vv. 36, 40, 44. The Kohathites of Eleazar's generation must have been made up of the descendants of Ishar and Uzziel, each of whom had three sons, consequently since all the Kohathites of Eleazar's generation were numbered at 2750, Num. iv. 36, it follows that these *six* men must have had between them according to the Scripture story 2748 sons, and we must suppose about the same number of daughters."

We have failed in our object if we have not shown in the preceding chapter that there is no reliance whatever to be placed in Bishop Colenso's figures, inasmuch as there is no data upon which they can be founded. The Bishop says that Dan had *one* son and *only* one, the sole foundation for which assertion is, that the families of the tribe of Dan were reckoned from him (Hushim) only, as having been one of the seventy who went down into Egypt. In order to show the fallacy of the Bishop's figures we will simply state his argument, and contrast it with an exactly parallel case; thus—Dan in the first generation had one son, Hushim, and that he had *only* one son is proved by Numbers xxvi. 42. We now set forth the case of his brother Joseph, who had in the first generation *two* sons, Ephraim and Manasseh, and that he had *only* two is proved by Num. xxvi. 28, where only these two are mentioned; but in this latter case a clear and simple explanation is given in the Narrative itself, an explanation which there can be no difficulty whatever in applying to the cases of the Danites and the Levites also. In Gen. xlviii. 5, 6 (before quoted), we have this sufficient elucidation of all the circumstances, "Thy two sons, Ephraim and Manasseh, which were born unto thee in the land of Egypt, before I came unto thee into Egypt, are mine, as Reuben and Simeon they shall be mine. And thy issue which thou begettest (Heb. אֲשֶׁר־הוֹלַדְתָּ, thou hast begotten) after them, shall be thine, *and shall be called after the name of their brethren in their inheritance.*" So that here we have the rule clearly laid down as to all questions of their future genealogies, and a full and sufficient reason why no more names are mentioned. The objection that no other sons of Joseph are ever mentioned in Scripture, is met by *Aben Ezra*, who says that "as they took their heritage under their elder brethren, there was no necessity to name them;" and by *Nachmanides*, who maintains that "the words of the prophet (Jacob) would not be uttered in vain." *Rashbam* is still stronger in favour of the view that Joseph had other sons when these words were spoken, for he says "those thou hast begotten during my seventeen years in Egypt."

We see also from the above passage that every one of the sons of Jacob *may* have had many more sons after they went down into Egypt, and we see also a reason why there are no names mentioned, if such were the case. For the cases of Joseph, and of Dan and Levi are exactly parallel, there is no reasoning that can be applied to one case that cannot be equally applied to the others. And the reason given for the suppression of the names of Joseph's other children is sufficient to show us why the names of those of Dan *may* have been suppressed also. We may also recall to remembrance the further proof of the birth of more children to Joseph's brethren in Egypt, which is contained in Joseph's promise to his brethren:—" I will nourish you and your little ones," (Heb., little children.) Gen. l. 21. In order that the Bishop's figures should carry any weight with them, he must show that there were no children of Dan or Levi included in this promise; failing to do this, his figures are utterly worthless, a mere schoolboy amusement of working an entirely supposititious case. To render them of any practical value, he must prove, not assume, that Dan had no more sons after Hushim, or Levi after Gershon, Kohath or Merari. He must prove, not assume, that the known custom of adoption into the tribes was not practised by the families of Dan or Levi during the whole period of their residence in Egypt. He must also prove, that neither Dan or Levi had any daughters who were given in marriage to Egyptians during the same period, and as proof in these cases is simply impossible, the whole of the Bishop's elaborate calculations must fall to the ground.

To show the fallacy of the Bishop's arguing from the assumption that all the names are given we will simply state a case as it occurs in the Bible. The tribe of Zebulon consists genealogically of his three sons, in Genesis and Numbers; but in the account in 1 Chron. the tribe is not mentioned, therefore, upon the Bishop's mode of reasoning, it had become extinct. In strict parity of reasoning, the Bishop must argue the non-existence of three tribes, Zebulon, Dan, and Judah, that are unmentioned in the genealogical list in the Chronicles. Nor are these cases the only variations in the account of the genealogies in Genesis, Numbers, and Chronicles. In fact to understand the repetitions and changes, the additions and omissions that occur in these three accounts, an amount of knowledge is necessary that no known means exist of attaining to; but we are not therefore justified in assuming the falsehood of the accounts; since to do so would be to act upon the monstrous proposition, that our *ignorance* is to be the guage of truth or falsehood. The great purpose of the Holy Spirit having been accomplished in the preservation of the record of the genealogy of the Messiah ben David, subordinate matters have been allowed to occupy their relative positions, or to sink into complete oblivion, and, now, the curiosity of the neophyte and the patient study of the scholar are alike exercised in vain.

It is utterly useless and even misleading to endeavour to apply figures in the partially known cases before us in this chapter; in fact they are inadmissible as a test; they are out of court, having no *locus standi*, inasmuch as there is no ascertained basis upon which they can be applied.

CHAPTER XIX.

Consists of the remarks of Commentators on the foregoing subject.

"CHAPTER XX.

"THE NUMBER OF PRIESTS AT THE EXODUS COMPARED WITH THEIR DUTIES, AND WITH THE PROVISION MADE FOR THEM." There is no quotation to this chapter, but the Bishop's statement runs as follows:—" The Book of Leviticus is chiefly occupied in giving directions to the Priests for the proper discharge of the different duties of their office, and further directions are given in the Book of Numbers. And now let us ask, for all the multifarious duties during the forty years' sojourn in the wilderness, for all the burnt-offerings, meat-offerings, peace-offerings, sin-offerings, trespass offerings, thank-offerings, etc., of a population like that of the city of LONDON, besides the daily and extraordinary sacrifices—how many priests were there? And the answer is very simple. There were only *three;* Aaron (till his death), and his two sons, Eleazar and Ithamar. And it is laid down very solemnly in Num. iii. 10, 'Thou shalt appoint Aaron and his sons, and they shall wait on the priest's office, and the stranger that cometh nigh shall be put to death.' So again, v. 38, 'Aaron and his sons, keeping charge of the sanctuary, and the stranger that cometh nigh shall be put to death.' Yet how was it possible that these two or three men should have discharged all these duties for such a vast multitude?

"The single work of offering the double sacrifice for women after childbirth must have utterly overpowered three Priests, though engaged without cessation from morning to night."

Our duty in this case is very simple, being merely to ascertain whether the Scriptures will allow the statement of the case as the Bishop has thus put it before us. We believe, and shall endeavour to show, that the Bishop has fallen into two radical errors (to use an exceedingly charitable phrase). He does not even mention the work of the Levites throughout the chapter, and only incidentally alludes even to their existence, the allusion being confined to the circumstance that they had forty-eight cities assigned to them, but not a single word respecting the services they were to perform in return for this liberal provision; nor does he say one word of the existence of the ordinary priests of the tabernacle. But in order systematically to set aside the Bishop's objections, we shall divide them into two statements:—

I. There were only three priests to do all the work.

II. It was impossible they could accomplish it.

I. There were only three priests to do all the work.

All through this chapter it is plainly implied that the three whose names are mentioned were the only persons allowed to do any portion of the work of the sanctuary. The Bishop quotes, "And the stranger that cometh nigh shall be put to death." But he wisely declines attempting to prove that this phrase was applicable to the Levites. But we will first see how much of the work thus confined to the three priests by the Bishop, was in reality performed by the 8500 helpmates they had from the very commencement of the tabernacle service; and here we must remark that while all the work was done by the direction and on the responsibility of the priesthood, a very large portion of it was performed by the Levites, under the supervision of the priests.

The whole tribe of the Levites was specially set apart for the external and internal service of the sanctuary, Num. iii. 41. They were to be supported upon the offerings to the tabernacle, Num. xviii. 24. They were given to Aaron to be his servants, Num. iii. 9. They were to do the service in the tabernacle before Aaron, and before his sons, Num. viii. 22. They had charge of the dedicated things, offerings, and tithes, 2 Chron. xxxi. 12, 14. What was the precise nature of this service of the tabernacle, we are not informed, but it is evident from many parts of Scripture that it was of a description to lighten the burden of the priesthood as much as possible, inasmuch as they were empowered to offer all burnt sacrifices unto the LORD on the Sabbaths, on the new moons, and on the set feasts, 1 Chron. xxiii. 31. Rashi says that the duty of the Levites was to kill the animal, take the blood to the priest, and to bring such part of the offering as was to be burned to the priest at the altar. (Comment on Num. xviii.)

This being the efficient aid the Levites might render, let us see how many priests there were they could thus assist. "Three" at first, answers the Bishop, "and after Aaron's death only two." But let us hear Calmet: "Next to the Levites, but superior to them in dignity, were the ordinary *priests*, who were chosen from the family of Aaron exclusively. They served immediately at the altar, prepared the victims [it will be seen above that Rashi says the Levites might do this also], and offered the sacrifices. They kept up a perpetual fire on the altar of the burnt sacrifices, and also in the lamps of the golden candlesticks in the sanctuary; they kneaded the loaves of shew-bread, which they baked and offered on the golden altar in the sanctuary, and changed them every Sabbath day. Every day, morning and evening, a priest (who was appointed at the beginning of the week by lot) brought into the sanctuary a smoking censer of incense, which he set upon the golden table; and which on no account was to be kindled with strange fire, that is, with any fire but that which was taken from the altar of burnt-sacrifice, Lev. x. 1, 2. And as the number and variety of their functions required them to be well read in their law, in order that they might be able to judge of the various *legal* uncleannesses, etc., this circumstance caused them to be consulted as interpreters of the law, Hos. iv. 6; Mal. ii. 7; Lev. xiii. 2; Num. v. 14, 15; as well as judges of controversies, Deut. xxi. 5; xvii. 8—13. In the time of war their business was to carry the Ark of the Covenant, to sound the holy trumpets, and animate the army to the performance of its duties. To them also it belonged publicly to bless the people in the name of the Lord."

It will be seen from this quotation that the work specially assigned by the Bishop, to two or three priests, is stated by Calmet to have been performed by an indefinite number of the ordinary priests of the tabernacle in their usual course of service. But, the Bishop may object, this is not showing from the Narrative that there really existed more than two or three priests; we shall now, therefore, proceed to quote a passage from the Book of Joshua, which settles the whole question.

The Bishop says, after the death of Aaron there were only two priests; the Narrative says, " And Joshua rose early in the morning, and the priests took up the ark of the Lord, and *seven* priests bearing seven trumpets of rams' horns before the ark of the Lord, went on continually," Josh. vi. 12, 13. This one passage completely dissolves the Bishop's objection founded on his assertion that there were only two priests at this time, for the narrative says the priests " bore the ark;" we cannot allow less than four priests for this office, and beside these four, other seven are specially mentioned as blowing rams' horns. Nor is it open to the Bishop to object that these were not the priests who offered the sacrifices, for both the Hebrew and the English version use the same word translated, "priest" in both cases. The Bishop quotes to show who offered the sacrifices, Lev. i. 5. "And the priests, Aaron's sons," where the Hebrew is בְּנֵי אַהֲרֹן הַכֹּהֲנִים, and the same word is used in Josh. vi. 13, וְשִׁבְעָה הַכֹּהֲנִים "and seven priests." In this passage of Joshua, there are then at the very least *eleven* priests especially mentioned instead of the *two*, asserted by the Bishop, to constitute the whole number existing at this time. How many more there were at the time we cannot find stated, but that there were a great many is shown by the provision that is specially made for them. It may be remarked that this convincing and complete refutation is taken from the Book of Joshua, which the Bishop announces himself as having *critically examined*.

The second point for our consideration is, It was impossible the two or three priests could perform the work.

We will first consider the offerings of the women in childbirth, as on this point the Bishop is exceedingly precise, and absurd in proportion. He avers that the offering of the young pigeons must have been 500 a day, 250 burnt-offerings, and 250 sin-offerings, and afterwards, more particularly states, "they would have averaged 264 a day, and each priest would have had to eat daily more than 88 for his own portion 'in the most holy place.'"

Though it is not easy to see how 264 divided between 3, would give *more* than 88 each, yet this is certainly an astounding statement, and if it were in the Narrative, or could be fairly deduced from it, might be quoted as quite sufficient of itself to condemn it. But it is not there. The whole law for women in childbirth is contained in Lev. xii., and is thus stated, The woman is to be unclean for seven days, the child (if a son) is to be circumcised the eighth day; then after thirty-three days, the mother is to come before the priest, and bring two young pigeons, one for a burnt-offering and one for a sin-offering. Now, we are expressly told that as a whole, this law was never observed, during the sojourn in the Wilderness, for the chief provision in it, that of circumcision, was utterly neglected during the entire term.

We have therefore no right to assume, that even one single pigeon was ever offered by a woman in the Wilderness, and to insist that one part of the law was scrupulously observed, and the other systematically neglected, would be equally as absurd as the Bishop's imagining, of the three priests eating the proceeds of this law, which we are expressly informed, was never enforced during the whole of the sojourn of forty years.

That there were doves in the Wilderness is shown by the repeated references to the fact, not only in the Pentateuch, but in several of the other books of Scripture.

We thus see, that the chief offering to which the Bishop objects, was in all probability never offered at all; and now we will turn to the other parts of the provision to which the Bishop offers objection. In Lev. vii. 7, 10, 34, it is said, That the priest should have the *sin* and *trespass* offerings, and the skin of the burnt-offerings, with the meat-offerings, and the wave breast and heave shoulder of the peace-offerings. And the Bishop objects, "What an enormous provision was this for Aaron and his four, afterward two, sons and their families. They were to have the skins of the burnt-offerings, and the shoulder and breast, that is double breast of the peace-offerings of a congregation of two millions of people for the general use of their three families!"

Let us see how many persons were comprised in the term "families." There was, instead of three, an indefinite number of priests, as we have shown, having an equally indefinite number of wives amongst them, with their sons and their daughters, their servants and their wives, and their servants' children, every one of

F

whom is specially mentioned as entitled to eat of the portion of the priesthood, Lev. xxii. 10, 13. So that if there was a very large provision (which need not be denied), it is clear that there must have been also a large number of persons who were absolutely dependent upon it. And, finally, instead of the special provision for the males of the priesthood being confined to three, and afterwards two persons, it is not stated, and consequently not known, how many men were entitled, by birth, position, and labour, to eat of the food that had been graciously set apart for them by the Lord their God.

"CHAPTER XXI.

"THE PRIESTS AND THEIR DUTIES AT THE CELEBRATION OF THE PASSOVER." There is no quotation, but continuing the subject of the previous chapter, the Bishop asks:—"How did these three priests manage at the celebration of the Passover? We are told, 2 Chron. xxx. 16, xxxv. 11, that the people killed the Passover, but the priests *sprinkled the blood from their hands*, and the Levites flayed them. Hence, when they kept the second Passover under Sinai, Num. ix. 5, where we must suppose that 150,000 lambs were killed 'between the two evenings,' Ex. xii. 6, for the 2,000,000 of people, each priest must have had to sprinkle the blood of 50,000 lambs in about two hours, that is at the rate of about *four hundred lambs every minute for two hours together*.

"Beside which, in the time of Hezekiah and Josiah, when it was desired to keep the Passover strictly 'in such sort as it was written,' 2 Chron. xxx. 5; the lambs were manifestly killed in the Court of the Temple. We must suppose, then, that the Paschal lambs in the wilderness were killed in the Court of the Tabernacle, in accordance, in fact, with the strict injunctions of the Levitical law, that all burnt-offerings, peace-offerings, sin-offerings, and trespass-offerings should be killed before Jehovah at the door of the Tabernacle of the Congregation. How, in fact, could the Priests have sprinkled the blood at all, if this were not the case, that the animals were killed in the Court of the Tabernacle? But the area of that court contained only 1692 square yards, and could only have held, when thronged, about 5000 people. How then are we to conceive of 150,000 lambs being killed within it, by at least 150,000 people in the space of two hours, that is, *at the rate of* 1250 *lambs a minute?*"

It will be noticed in reading over the above statement of the Bishop, that the whole of it is founded upon supposition. "*We must suppose,*" says the Bishop, and he proceeds to carry out this very necessary proceeding, and build up the chapter upon it. But in order to render full justice, we must gather the Bishop's thoughts, surmises and suppositions, and shall state them in his own words.

Question. "How did these three priests manage at the celebration of the Passover?"

Assertion 1. "There were 150,000 lambs required."

Assertion 2. "The priests had to sprinkle the blood."

Assertion 3. "The lambs were killed in the Court of the Tabernacle."

Assertion 4. "There were only two hours in which they might be killed."

Question. "How did these three priests manage at the celebration of the Passover?"

The answer to this is as brief and concise as possible :—*There is not a single word or even a hint in the Narrative that they had anything whatever to do with it;* neither in the directions for the first Passover in Egypt, or in the accounts of the second under

Sinai, is there the slightest authorization for the priest, *as such*, to interfere with it, to assume any authority, or to take upon himself any responsibility as to the management. And this the Bishop evidently knew, but having to make out a case, if possible, in a Critical Examination of the Pentateuch, he has selected the record of an observance of the Passover, hundreds of years after the date of those books, and has assumed, without the slightest warrant for so doing, against the plain meaning of the text, that the circumstances of the two occasions were identical. The plain law of the Passover in Egypt, and also in the Wilderness under Sinai, was that it should be a separate household ordinance, in which the head of the family (if large enough, and if another family joined, a chosen deputy) should act as priest on the occasion. There is no priest named in either case; there are no duties indicated for him to perform, and the law that the Passover was to be offered in "the place that the Lord their God should choose," was not promulgated for many years after the second Passover had been observed; nor is there the slighest hint of the knowledge or practice of such a centralizing law with regard to the Passover in any part of the narrative, co-incident with the times of either the first or second Passover; so that the whole of the objection insinuated under the form of this first question is completely dissolved.

Assertion 1. "There were 150,000 lambs required."

We have examined this assertion before, but as it is a pet point of the Bishop's, reiterated again and again, we will here devote a little more attention to it. The lamb was to be "a male of the first year without blemish." The carcase of such a lamb, "with his head and his legs, and the purtenance thereof," will weigh about thirty-five pounds. The Bishop's calculation is founded upon the supposition of fifteen persons to one lamb, therefore each person in a feast eaten in haste, was to have, according to the Bishop's estimate, two pounds and five ounces of meat (with the bone included), beside unleavened bread and bitter herbs; and it must not be forgotten, that the same amount is calculated for even the little children; that is, a meal for a little child was to be, according to the Bishop, two pounds weight of solid meat, with bread and vegetables, and it was to be eaten in haste, and ready prepared for an immediate journey. The Bishop uses the word "preposterous" in the course of his objections to the Bible, we venture to offer it for consideration as fitly describing his own estimate.

The Bishop may object, "This estimate is founded on the average of Josephus;" but Josephus does not speak in reference to the observances in Egypt, or under Sinai, but of a time many hundreds of years afterward, when the long enjoyment of the possession of a "land flowing with milk and honey," might render such a liberal provision perfectly easy. The Bishop takes the estimate given for a special purpose just before the destruction of Jerusalem, and without, by a single word, pointing out the difference of the times and circumstances, uses the estimate of Josephus for both Egypt and Sinai, and leaves his reader to believe that Josephus spoke of those times also.

Again, the most notable observance of the Passover that is related, occurred in the days of King Josiah, when it is stated, 2 Chron. xxxv. 18, "There was no Passover like to that, kept in Israel from the days of Samuel the prophet, neither did all the kings of Israel keep such a passover as Josiah kept, and the priests and the Levites, and all Judah and Israel that were present, and the inhabitants of Jerusalem."

The number of lambs required for this Passover is expressly stated, as they were given by the king himself, and the princes, priests, and Levites. The king gave thirty thousand, the princes gave two thousand six hundred, and the priests and Levites five thousand; so that for the grandest passover celebration that was ever known, after the people had come into their inheritance, and when they had greatly multiplied in number, the number of passover lambs was 37,600, 2 Chron. xxxv. instead of the 150,000 said to be required by Bishop Colenso.

Assertion 2. "The priests had to sprinkle the blood."

This also is simple assumption, and it is assumed in order to raise an objection afterward, but there is not a word in the Narrative that will warrant such a statement. The law of the Passover would be fully and properly observed, though no priest ever saw the lamb, though it was killed in any part of the Camp; nor need any of the blood be sprinkled by any priest whatever.

We have only to quote the words of the Bishop's own volume, to show that he has not a shadow of authority for his statement, for the Bishop writes, quoting from Kurtz, "*It is nowhere stated* that on the occasion of the first festival in commemoration of the Exodus *the lambs were slaughtered at the sanctuary*, or that the blood either was, or was to be, sprinkled upon the altar, nor is there any notice of the services of the priests being required." "*It is nowhere expressly commanded* in the Pentateuch that the blood of the paschal lambs was (to be) sprinkled on the altar by the priests." And in reply to the Bishop's assertion that it was necessary to sprinkle the blood of 400 lambs a minute for two hours together, we may simply ask for any passage of God's Word to show that even one single Passover lamb was ever brought to the door of the Tabernacle of the Congregation. If then it is nowhere expressly commanded that the priests should sprinkle the blood of the paschal lambs, and nowhere stated that they did so, why does the Bishop assert that each priest must have had to sprinkle the blood of 50,000 lambs in about two hours?

Writing such as this is the very mockery of criticism, resulting from deep-seated determination to destroy, by any means, however questionable, our confidence in the truth and authority of the Scriptures of the living God.

Assertion 3. "The lambs were killed in the Court of the Tabernacle."

It is nowhere stated that this was done; but the Bishop cites the cases of the burnt-offering, Lev. i. 3, 5, and the sin-offering, Lev. iii. 2, and he argues that because these were offered at the door of the Tabernacle of the Congregation, therefore the passover lambs must have been slain in the same place; but there is no parallelism in the cases to warrant the assumption; the burnt-offering and the sin-offering were *commanded* to be offered at the door of the tabernacle, it was an essential part of the sacrifice that they should be offered at that particular place; there was no other place where they could legitimately be offered. But it formed no part of the law of the Passover in Exodus that the lambs should be slain in any particular spot, nor is there (as before mentioned) any indication of any place of offering in the account of the second Passover. Moreover, in the cases of the burnt-offering and the peace-offering the first was to be wholly, and the second partially disposed of, by burning before the LORD. But no part of the Passover was consecrated for any such purpose, even the sprinkling of the blood was to be a "*token*," not an *offering*. The *priest* must sprinkle the blood of the burnt offering, "and the stranger that cometh nigh shall be put to death;" but of the Passover lamb it is said, "The whole assembly of the congregation of Israel shall kill it in the evening; and *they* shall take of the blood and strike it on the two side posts." Thus while in the one case, the most solemn portion of the service was restricted to the priests, with the penalty of death for disobedience, in the other the head of the family was authorized and directed to perform it in person. It is almost incredible that these simple but wide distinctions should have escaped the notice of the Bishop when professedly engaged in a Critical Examination: but they either did so, or they did not; if they did escape his notice, they settle the question of his ability to enter into a critical examination; if they did not, but were suppressed; they equally decide the question of the honesty of his intention in writing his so-called criticism.

There is neither assertion, nor proof, nor probability in the Narrative which the Bishop can bring forward to warrant the conclusion to which he comes, or to support the assertion that he has made, that the lambs were killed in the Court of the Tabernacle.

The confused jumbling together of different times and places in the first paragraph of this chapter, is good evidence how hard the Bishop was put to it to obtain the merest semblance of authority for the absurd calculations which follow after. He says: "We are told in 2 Chron. xxx. 16, xxxv. 11, that the people killed the Passover, but the priests sprinkled the blood from their hands, and the Levites flayed them." (How many priests, how many *courses of priests* were present at the time mentioned?) The Bishop gives no answer to such questions, but jumps back without any notice to Num. ix. 5, and the three priests of his own imagination, and proceeds to imagine that these three were to do the same work as all the indefinite number of priests employed at the grand Passover in the time of Josiah the king, and he admits afterwards, *It is nowhere stated* that the priests were to lay even so much as a finger upon the work.

Assertion 4. "There were only two hours in which the Passover lambs might be killed."

This assertion is several times repeated in different parts of the book, and we shall here therefore clearly state the real time that was allowed. The Narrative in Exodus says,—" Kill it in the evening," (translated in the margin, Heb., *between the two evenings*). When this time was according to hours of the day, is not stated either there or elsewhere that we have been able to find. We shall therefore seek out Jewish authority as carrying the most weight with it. The Jewish day consisted of only two parts, morning and evening; till the sun passed the meridian all was morning, after that, evening. The first evening with the Jews began just after twelve o'clock and continued till sunset; their second evening began at sunset and continued through the whole of the twilight. Between twelve o'clock, therefore, and the end of twilight, the Passover Lamb was to be slain. Dr. Cox, in his "Biblical Antiquities" (Ency. Met.), p. 180, says: "They distinguished also between the two evenings, the first beginning at noon, and reaching to the setting of the sun, the second commencing at sunset, and the space from noon to sunset they called *Been haarabeem;* *i.e.,* between the two evenings." Now, at the very earliest computation, it would not be the end of twilight at the close of March in Judea before six o'clock; and as the whole of this time is between the two evenings, it follows that there were six instead of two hours in which the Passover might be killed, or in other words, just three times as long as the Bishop has allowed.

In leaving the Bishop's assertions, assumptions, and suppositions in this chapter with the foregoing answers, we would merely remark; if this is to be the method by which men of any sense who love the Scriptures are to have their belief in the Bible destroyed, it is a task beyond the Bishop's well known powers of calculation, to set forth the time that will be occupied in carrying out such a purpose.

"CHAPTER XXII.

"THE WAR IN MIDIAN." There is no quotation, but the Bishop states his case as follows: "We have now concluded our preliminary work of pointing out some of the most prominent inconsistencies and impossibilities which exist in the story of the Exodus as it lies before us in the Pentateuch; and we have surely exhibited enough to relieve the mind from any superstitious dread in pursuing further the consideration of the question. I believe that to the great majority of my readers many of the above facts will be as new as I freely admit they were to myself till within a comparatively recent period." The Bishop proceeds to fall foul of "Aids to Faith" and "Replies to Essays and Reviews," and especially of Professor Rawlinson; but as we have not yet discovered the relation those volumes bear to the truth of the Pentateuch, we shall pass his remarks. He next attacks the veracity of the Hebrew numerals in the books of Judges and Chronicles, a proceeding which is rather out of place, in our opinion, in a Critical Examination of the Pentateuch, and we shall therefore decline to follow him. But he returns again to the 600,000 on foot, and insists (which nobody denies) that this number is so completely interwoven in the narrative that it cannot be taken out or touched without destroying it. As we fully believe the number to be correct, and consequently have no wish to alter it, we may pass on to the Bishop's remarks. "These things we have all along been looking at, as it were, from a distant point of view, through a misty atmosphere, dreading, it may be, some of us, to approach and gaze more closely on the truth itself." We will only say in passing that this strikes us as consummately cool. The Bishop owns that he has never hitherto given his Bible a thoughtful and attentive study, and claims an indefinite number of companions in carelessness. But while we admit the candour of the Bishop's confession of his own shortcomings, we must protest against being included in the listless number. We love our Bible history, we have passed many years of close and happy study as pupils and teachers in Working Men's Bible Classes, and so far from dreading to look into the Bible, we will relate our experience while writing this refutation. *We have found that the best way to answer the Bishop's objections is to search out the minute information contained in the Book itself.* We have gathered some small portion of the information, as will, we hope, be seen; but our time is very limited; we have, however, discovered enough to convince us, that if any man of average capacity and sufficient leisure will give his mind to the task, he will be able to dissolve all the Bishop's objections by the simple quotation of appropriate scriptures, without adding a word of his own.

In short, *the Bible will defend itself* against any number of such attacks as those in the puerile criticism before us.

We pass now to consider the main incident of this chapter—the war in Midian—which is thus stated by the Bishop: "How thankful we must be that we are no longer obliged to believe as a matter of fact of vital consequence to our eternal hope, the story related in Numb. xxxi., where we are told that a force of 12,000 Israelites slew *all* the males of the Midianites, took captive *all* the females and children, seized *all* their cattle and flocks (72,000 oxen, 61,000 asses, 675,000 sheep), and *all* their goods, and burnt *all* their cities, and *all* their goodly castles, without the loss of a single man; and then, by the command of Moses, butchered in cold blood all the women and children, 'except all the women children who have not known a man by lying with him.' These last the Israelites were to 'keep for themselves.' They amounted, we are told, to 32,000 (v. 35), mostly, we must suppose, under the age of sixteen or eighteen. We may fairly reckon that there were as many more under the age of forty, and half as many more above forty, making altogether 80,000 females, of whom, according to the story, Moses ordered 48,000 to be killed, besides (say) 20,000 young boys. The tragedy of Cawnpore, where 300 were butchered, would sink into nothing when compared with such a massacre, if indeed we were required to believe it. And these 48,000 females must have represented 48,000 men, all of whom, in that case, we must also believe to have been killed, their property pillaged, their castles demolished, and towns destroyed, by 12,000 Israelites, who, in addition, must have carried off 100,000 captives (more than eight persons to each man), and driven before them 808,000 head of cattle (more than sixty-seven for each man), and all without the loss of a single man. How is it possible to quote the Bible as in any way condemning slavery when we read here, v. 40, of 'Jehovah's tribute' of slaves, 'thirty-two persons?'"

Gathering up, first, the incidents of the war itself from the Bishop's statements, they are as follows : that 12,000 men attacked and conquered 48,000 others, and that they slew them and took a vast amount of spoil—and that this account is incredible, unhistorical, and untrue.

To show the futility of the Bishop's objection we shall simply quote a passage from the history of our own land—a record of the battle of Plassey, which we find in Lord Macaulay's "Lord Clive," Trav. Lib., part ii. pp. 47, 48. "The day broke, the day which was to decide the fate of India. At sunrise the army of the nabob, pouring through many openings of the camp, began to move towards the grove where the English lay. *Forty thousand* infantry armed with firelocks, pikes, swords, bows and arrows, covered the plain. They were accompanied by fifty pieces of ordnance of the largest size, each tugged by a long team of white oxen, and each pushed on from behind by an elephant. Some smaller guns, under the direction of a few French auxiliaries, were perhaps more formidable. The cavalry were *fifteen thousand*, drawn, not from the effeminate population of Bengal, but from the bolder race which inhabits the northern provinces, and the practised eye of Clive could perceive that both the men and the horses were more powerful than those of the Carnatic. The force which he had to oppose to this great multitude consisted of only *three thousand* men. But of these nearly a thousand were English, and all were led by English officers, and trained in the English discipline. Conspicuous in the ranks of the little army were the men of the 39th Regiment, which still bears on its colours, amidst many honourable additions won under Wellington in Spain and Gascony, the name of Plassey, and the proud motto, *Primus in Indis*.

"The battle commenced with a cannonade. In an hour the forces of Surajah Dowlah were dispersed, never to reassemble. Only five hundred of the vanquished were slain. But their camp, their guns, their baggage, innumerable waggons, innumerable cattle, remained in the power of the conquerors. With the loss of twenty-two soldiers killed and fifty wounded, Clive had scattered an army of near sixty thousand men, and subdued an empire larger and more populous than Great Britain."

It will be seen from the above quotation that while Bishop Colenso asserts it to be incredible that 12,000 attacked and conquered 48,000; Lord Macaulay distinctly states that Clive's force consisted of only 3000 against nearly 60,000. In the "incredible" instance, the proportion is 1 against 4, in the "historical" instance, 1 against 20. So also of the spoil. It is "incredible" that 12,000 should capture 100,000; it is "historical" that 3000 subdued as large a population as that of Great Britain, consisting of many millions. It is "incredible" that 808,000 cattle were part of the prey. It is "historical" that *innumerable* waggons and *innumerable* cattle remained in the power of the conquerors. Will the Bishop assert that Macaulay's statement (so much more wonderful than the Bible narrative) is unhistorical? Will he say that the inscription on the colours of the 39th Regiment commemorates an action that never took place?

We might instance, also, the battle of Morgarten in Switzerland, when the cantons of Uri, Schwytz, and Unterwalden, mustering only 1600 men in all, defeated and drove out of their country an Austrian force of 20,000 men. Here, again, instead of 1 to 4 is 1 to 10; will the Bishop declare it unhistorical and untrue?

It is apparent that these battles far exceed the Bible narrative of the war in Midian in results proportioned to means, and the Bishop must disprove *all* the circumstances related of both these battles before he can hope to establish his assertion of the "incredibility" of the Scripture Narrative.

But another of the Bishop's objections is the impossibility of driving away the spoil; to which the answer is simple and easy. When the Midianite men were slain there would be no obstacle to the victors employing the women and lads to drive away the cattle, the women in Eastern countries being accustomed to tending on flocks and herds.

The third objection is to the wholesale slaughter in cold blood after the battle.

The purpose of this war was national extermination; this nation had filled up the measure of its iniquity, sentence had gone forth, the swords of the Israelites were the appointed means of vengeance; and however terrible the slaughter outside the camp may have been, it is idle to say that it is incredible or that we have no right to imagine Our Father as ordering or sanctioning it, when every generation a thousand millions perish.

But these Midianites died in a manner so horrible!

Was this manner of death more horrible than that of the victims of the Black Death in Europe in 1350 A.D., which destroyed millions of human beings—100,000 persons dying in the city of Florence alone; and which in every place it visited carried off, in seven or eight months, one third of the population?

Was this visitation of war more terrible than the destructions and slaughters of the earthquake and the volcano have been? Think of the destruction of Antioch by an earthquake in 526 A.D. That great city, crowded with inhabitants and strangers gathered on a festive occasion, was suddenly startled on a calm day, by the earth rocking and heaving beneath their feet, and in a few moments 250,000 of them are buried by falling houses, or the earth opening and swallowing them up. In the year 17 A.D. no less than thirteen cities in Asia Minor were, in like manner, overwhelmed in a single night. The sun had just dissipated the fog on a warm calm morning in Lisbon, in 1755, when suddenly subterranean heaving and thundering began; and in six minutes the city was a heap of ruins, and 60,000 of the inhabitants were numbered among the dead. Kircher has also left us a thrilling account of the destruction of the city of Euphemia in Calabria, in 1638, when 5000 persons perished. "After some time," he says, "the violent paroxysm of the earthquake ceasing, I looked for Euphemia, and saw only a frightful black cloud. When this had cleared away nothing but a dismal and putrid lake was to be seen where the city had once stood." In like manner did Port Royal, in the West Indies, sink beneath the waters, with nearly all its inhabitants in less than one minute, in the year 1692.

In the presence of natural destruction on so vast, sudden, and terrific a scale as the foregoing instances record, it is idle to object that God would not employ even exterminating war to accomplish purposes which He saw to be righteous and just. These Midianites were idolaters; they had nearly ruined Israel by drawing them into the same awful snare. This was Jehovah's quarrel, and it was at His express command this unsparing destruction took place. He had created them, they had sinned horribly against Him; and the lives He had given He had a perfect right to dispose of in any way that seemed to Him best.

The Bishop concludes this last chapter of objections with some chronological notices of the transactions of six months which he says are incredible, and which we will now rapidly pass in review.

I. We are told "that Aaron died on the first day of the fifth month of the fortieth year of the wanderings, and they mourned for him *a month*." And, as the Bishop concludes, without a shadow of authority in the Narrative, they did nothing *but* mourn during this first month of the six.

II. "After this, 'Arad the Canaanite fought against Israel and took some of them prisoners; whereupon the Israelites attacked these Canaanites and utterly destroyed them and their cities,' for which two transactions we may allow another *month*."

It is not stated in the Heb. or Sept. that the destruction, though denounced, was consummated at this time; the Heb. is וַיַּחֲרֵם "devoted to destruction," and the LXX have και ανεθεματισεν, "anathematized," or "devoted to destruction;" but the destruction did not take place till some time afterward, see Josh. xv. 14; so that this month may be struck out altogether.

III. "They then 'journeyed from Mount Hor, by way of the Red Sea, to compass the land of Edom, and the people murmured and were plagued with fiery serpents,' etc.; for all which we must allow a *fortnight*."

IV. "They now marched and made *nine* encampments, Num. xxi. 10—20; for which we cannot well allow less than *a month* (with three days' rest between each encampment)."

The Bishop here falls into an error, fatal to any pretension to careful examination. There are only *four* encampments mentioned in the verses indicated—*i.e.*, Oboth, Ije-abarim, Zared, and Arnon, v. 10—13; the remainder of the verses, 14—20, are simply an extract from the "Book of the Wars of the Lord," and the Bishop has mistaken the end of the extract for the continuation of the Narrative, which recommences in v. 21. A simple examination of the parallel passage in chap. xxxiii. would have saved him from this mis-statement. We must, however, subtract the largest half of the month the Bishop claims in this case also.

V. "They then 'sent messengers to Sihon, king of the Amorites, who gathered all his people together and fought against Israel,' etc.; for which we must allow another *month*."

VI. "After that 'Moses sent to spy out Jaazer, and they took the villages thereof, and drove out the Amorites that were there,' say in another *fortnight*."

VII. "Then they 'turned up by way of Bashan; and Og, the king of Bashan, went out against them, and they smote him . . . and possessed his land;' for all this we must allow at the very least *a month*."

The order here stated belongs to the Bishop, who has manufactured it for his purpose. The words in V. "They *then ;*" in VI. "*After* that ;" and in VII. "*Then* they turned"—all belong to the Bishop, there is nothing of the sort in the Narrative. We shall not strain the text in the least by assuming that all these last three were cotemporaneous, and instead of occupying ten weeks might have been done in a third of that time; and thus, instead of six months being required, half the time would have sufficed. Thus leaving ample time for the events detailed in the conclusion of the Book of Numbers, some of which may have been cotemporaneous also—viz., the march to the plains of Moab; Balak's intercourse with Balaam; Israel abiding in Shittim and committing whoredom with the daughters of Moab; the consequent plague; the numbering of the people and the Midianite war; the first and second, the third and fourth, and the fifth and sixth of these, may very possibly have in each case taken place together; and thus considered, in the absence of a word to the contrary in the Narrative, the Bishop's last objection is as untenable, as easily set aside, as his first and all that have followed; for we think we have fairly answered them all.

G

"CHAPTER XXIII.

"CONCLUDING REMARKS." No quotation. The Bishop writes: "Having thus been impelled to take an active part in showing the groundlessness of that notion of Scripture Inspiration, which so many have long regarded as the very foundation of their faith and hope, a demand may be made upon me for something to supply the loss—for something to fill up the aching void which will undoubtedly be felt at first, when *that* faith which has been built wholly or mainly upon the basis of the historical truth of the Pentateuch, must be in danger of collapsing together with its support. In the present stage of the discussion it is impossible for me to answer fully, as I would to such a demand, though I trust to be enabled to do so before my work is brought to its close."

The Bishop proceeds to offer his own Commentary on the Epistle to the Romans as the best stop-gap he has to propose, and says he has there "rightly explained the apostle's own meaning, and have expressed truly, as it seems to me, the manner in which he himself would have adapted his teaching to the circumstances, social and intellectual, of the present day. The main essence of that teaching is, that our righteousness is wholly of faith, a living trust in God's love; that we *must* all, and we *may* all depend entirely on our Father's mercy, and come as children to his footstool continually for light and life, for help and glory, for counsel and guidance, and, if need be, for that 'loving correction' which shall 'make us great.' That essential principle of St. Paul's teaching remains still an eternal truth for our strength and consolation, whatever may be the effect of the view taken of the Mosaic history upon other parts of the current belief of Christendom." The Bishop then reviews the difficulties of missionaries, and suggests that his new theory will allow them to cut and carve the Scriptures so as to meet the early prejudices of the heathen they go forth to instruct. He also sketches the mode in which we are to teach our children in the future : " Let us teach them at once to know that they are not to look for the inspiration of the Holy One, which breathes through its pages, in respect of any such matters of these which the writers wrote as men, with the same liability to error from any cause as other men. Let us rather teach them to look for the sign of God's Spirit speaking to them in the Bible . . to the reason and conscience. Thus, for instance, we may lead them to recognize the fact, that the third and sixth chapters of Exodus, which declare to us the name of God—I AM—whether written by Moses or any other fellow-man, were written by one who was specially inspired, first, to conceive himself the transcendent, divine thought, and then express it to others. . . . . It matters not that the writer may have exhibited the living truth in the clothing of human imagery, and embodied the divine lesson which his own mind had received, and which he felt himself commissioned to impart to his fellow-men, in the story of the flaming bush and the audible voice. This circumstance would not at all affect the nature of the truth itself, which remains still eternally true, whatever be the form in which it is announced to us ; just as the truths which our Lord himself teaches are not the less true because clothed in the imagery of a parable or of a narrative (like that of Dives and Lazarus, or of the good Samaritan), which we do not suppose to be historically true.

" But then, too, they must be taught to recognize the voice of God's Spirit in whatever way, by whatever ministry, he vouchsafes to speak to the children of men, and to realize the solid comfort of the thought, that not in the Bible only, but also out of the Bible ; not to us Christians only, but to our fellow-men of all climes and countries, ages and religions, the same gracious

Teacher is revealing, in different measures, according to his own good pleasure, the hidden things of God."

It is very plain, judging from these concluding remarks, that the Bishop has written himself into the belief of the invincible nature of his objections, and that they will be sufficient to overthrow in others, all faith in the truth and authority of God's Word. That, on the faith of his assertions and assumptions, on the strength of a few mere objections, without allowing any weight to the incalculable mass of affirmative evidence, we shall at once abandon our old and tried mode of belief. That on an *ex parte* statement of one side of a very minute portion of an almost infinite question, we are ready to give up our Bible, and trust ourselves to—what? Clearly the Bishop does not know himself, or so distrusts his purposed substitute, that he is afraid to let it see the light. We are to trust to a vague and misty promise of a substitute at the end of Bishop Colenso's work, which is to consist of an indefinite number of parts, to be published at an indefinite period.

The consummate folly of the expectation is equalled by the consummate self-conceit of the promise. Here is a man promising to reconstruct our Bibles, every chapter in whose short book is full of errors, who leaves out an important word in the very first text he touches; who tells us gravely that 264 divided amongst three gives *more* than eighty-eight for each; who says there were *nine* encampments where there were only *four*, and who quotes one half of a verse that can be made to appear to favour his theory, and who leaves out the other half, which utterly destroys it. This is the man who comes forward and tells us that all our great English scholars have been in error in believing the inspiration of the Bible; that Newton, and Locke, and Clarke, and Lightfoot, Van Mildert, and Walton, and a glorious army of others, have all been mistaken, and their mistake has been detected by a very cursory examination of about a dozen texts of Scripture. We are to give up our Bibles at the bidding of one who evidently does not know what he himself believes— who did not foresee the mass of contradictions and absurdities the first onset of really competent and hostile criticism has exposed in his ridiculous theory. A man who never once could have looked fairly into *the bases upon which his calculations are founded*, or he *must* have discovered they were not trustworthy.

But there is another supposition. Suppose us willing to give up our view of the Bible, and accept the Bishop's promised substitute, and he dies or changes his mind again, where shall we be then? with our old hope gone, and in its place nothing but a Commentary on a part of the Bible, which part has gone in the common wreck; for with very strange logic, or the inconsistency of madness, the Bishop earnestly recommends his Commentary, after having (in imagination at least) destroyed the authority of the Text upon which it is founded. In the name of common-sense, why recommend the Commentary when the Text is gone? surely there can be no wild expectation that the Commentary will do very well in the place of the Text itself.

After these samples we may well believe the Bishop is a wise man, thoroughly competent to re-edit St. Paul's Epistles, and to tell us what St. Paul would have taught if he were now living amongst us. Firstly, according to the Bishop, he would not teach what he did teach most emphatically when (fortunately for us) he was allowed to speak for himself—that "all Scripture is given by inspiration of God"—for his new expositor asserts, "that is a mistaken view that must be done away with, and my book shall do it." Secondly, he would leave out this denunciation, "There be some that would trouble you, and would pervert the gospel of Christ. But though we or an angel from heaven preach any other gospel unto you than that we have preached unto you, let him be accursed." Since if this be not omitted, some of us might think it a very severe personality on the Commentator himself, and his mode of dealing with the Bible. But on what authority does the Bishop state that Paul would *adapt* his teaching, when the Spirit of Him who spake through Paul is " the same yesterday, to-day, and for ever ?" There is one thing we may say with certainty that Paul would not do, he would neither ignore nor keep back the name of Him who was ever foremost in Paul's thoughts and words; for whom he had "suffered the loss of all things, and do count them but dung, that I may win Christ and be found in Him." If Paul were now living, he would trumpet forth, " Christ, the power of God, and the wisdom of God ;" not, as the Bishop has done, broadly insinuate that the Lord of glory might be mistaken even after He rose from the dead. Paul would teach now as of old, and, thank God, there are thousands of us who would welcome the teacher and the teaching with assenting hearts, that " Christ Jesus, of God, is made unto us wisdom and righteousness, and sanctification and redemption." "Who ever hardened himself against Him and prospered" ?

But not only would Paul teach differently, according to the Bishop; we pass to something worse, something which, coming from a Christian minister, is horrible and infamous; our Lord taught that " which we do not suppose to be historically true."

Speaking for yourself, Bishop, you have a right to suppose what you please, but pause before thrusting yourself forward, unasked and most unwelcome, as the expositor of the ideas of your Christian countrymen. We believe that our Lord never uttered a single word that was not strictly true in every sense of the word. We know that He spake in Parables, it is yet to be shown that every one of the incidents therein mentioned were not the strictly truthful record of actual facts. Where is the proof that the incident of the good Samaritan never took place exactly as it is recorded? We believe that it did really occur, and that our Lord narrated a fact, not imagined a fable: so also with the rich man and Lazarus, we believe that there also our Lord is recording facts in the eternal life-history of both men, that the state of felicity spoken of by our Lord as Abraham's bosom, really existed then if it does not now, and we know that so the Jews understood his speech, from the fact that Josephus has left us a full exposition of what the Jews understood of, and characterized as, being in Abraham's bosom.

But not only our Lord, and his loved and faithful servant Paul, but the writer of the Pentateuch is also to be set right, and re-introduced to us in an entirely new character; in which no one would be more astonished and dismayed to see him than he would be to find himself; for we are told that some of his words are true, others are not true. That the revelation of the I AM, is a grand and solemn truth set between two falsehoods; first, a falsehood, the burning bush; second, a truth, the revelation of God; then another falsehood, the audible voice. And this contemptible trash is submitted for the consideration and adoption of men who have learned to read and to think! Where is the authority to tell us which is which, to point out to us why we should believe the central and hardest part of the whole, and reject the far easier first and last. Our reason is to be our guide? We have only to see where reason, untaught and unaided, guides savages and cannibals, to reject the offer with contempt and scorn. But conscience will help! No, we are warned against trusting to that which is itself unsound; for conscience is seared; in short, "the natural man," to which the Bishop would relegate us, "understandeth not the things that be of God, neither can he know them, because they are spiritually discerned;" but "God hath revealed them unto us by his Spirit," in his Holy Word.

If we are to judge of the Bishop's new religion by the outline of what it may perhaps be, he has given us in this last chapter, it appears to be; that we are to draw nigh to God, confident in our own merits, and accepted through them; for there is not a word or a hint of coming to God *through Jesus Christ*, in all the shameful and deistical pages.

We, sinners, are to come into the presence of the holy Almighty God, and to find acceptance and blessing in Our Father's love; when God is angry with the wicked every day. He is a consuming fire; of too pure eyes to behold iniquity, shall we, born in it, and ruined by it, dare of ourselves and by ourselves, to come before Him? Nay, but in the loved name of the spotless Lamb of God, the beloved and only begotten of the Father, full of grace and truth, the Daysman between God and sinning men; so must we come, to appear acceptably before Our Father who is in heaven.

Not with the Pantheism of the Bishop of Natal; not with the words, however noble, of the man who trained his own son so badly that he became the greatest drunkard in Rome; not with the dim natural religion of the Gooroo, who knew nothing of God in Christ forgiving iniquity, transgression, and sin; nor with the depressing and awful fatalism of the Bishop's last recommendation, but in Christ and like Him; "standing fast in the liberty wherewith He has made us free;" proving all things, holding fast that which is good—the good Word of God; knowing that in us, that is in our flesh, dwelleth no good thing; trusting wholly and alone upon Jesus; passing from faith to faith, strength to strength, glory to glory, even as by the Spirit of the Lord, till we all come, in the fulness of the blessing of the gospel of the grace of God in Christ, to our true place in the universe of God, our eternal home with Him in heaven, through the death and passion of Jesus Christ our Lord.

HABRILD, Printer, LONDON.

THE BIBLE IN THE WORKSHOP.

PART II.

THE
BIBLE IN THE WORKSHOP.

PART II.

A REFUTATION

OF

THE SECOND PART OF BISHOP COLENSO'S CRITICAL
EXAMINATION OF THE PENTATEUCH
AND BOOK OF JOSHUA.

THE AGE AND AUTHORSHIP OF THE PENTATEUCH CONSIDERED.

BY TWO WORKING MEN,
A JEW AND A GENTILE.

Τί γὰρ, εἰ ἠπίστησάν τινες;
Μὴ ἡ ἀπιστία αὐτῶν τὴν πίστιν τοῦ Θεοῦ καταργήσει.
PAUL. (Rom. iii. 3.)

LONDON:
W. KENT & CO., PATERNOSTER ROW.

HARRILD, PRINTER, LONDON.

ADVERTISEMENT.

The favour which has been accorded to the First Part of this Refutation has emboldened the writers to proceed with this review of the Second Part of the Bishop of Natal's work.

They cannot but feel the compliment implied in the doubt that has been so often expressed as to the former Part having been written by Mechanics. But they wish to add, that neither the Publishers nor themselves would be parties to any deception. They have neither sought nor received help from any one in writing this Refutation.

PREFACE.

THE Bishop of Natal, in commencing the preface of his Second Part, states:—"My former book has had, I believe, the effect which I desired."

If a storm of reprobation, like that which has greeted the Bishop's volume from every possible quarter—from Jews and Christians, Churchmen and Dissenters, Scholars and Mechanics, City-missionaries, and Scripture-readers—be a desirable thing from the Bishop's point of view; it is indisputable that his desire has been gratified, for we do not remember such remarkable unanimity of feeling, such perfect accord of reprobation and condemnation on any subject that has ever occupied the attention of the religious public.

Rabbins have mocked, in written letters to newspapers, at the Bishop's transparent assumption of Hebrew scholarship. Churchmen have pointed out the errors in his reasoning, and have animadverted upon the Bishop's proceedings abroad, in order to account for his conduct at home. Dissenters have flouted his absurd claims to infallibility of judgment, asking whether Dr. Colenso had not better proclaim himself Pope in England at once; and Mechanics have laughed while at their work at the ridiculous nature of some of the arguments he has set forth.

We shall, therefore, venture to assert, that such perfect unanimity of condemnatory judgment has never previously been displayed upon any public question in the history of the modern religious world.

The Bishop says, also, that he asked, and has obtained, attention on the part of the "thoughtful and intelligent among the Laity."

There can be no doubt that thoughtful attention has been given,—and with what result? As far as we can ascertain, the general opinion of all who have read the first book is that it is an utter, complete failure; that there is not in it a single argument that need inflict a moment's uneasiness on any timid mind; and that the absurd and wicked view of the knowledge possessed by the Lord Jesus, is an indelible disgrace to him who placed it on record as his deliberate opinion, while retaining his position in the English Church.

This appeal to the laity is followed by a declaration that the mouths of the doctors and clergy of the Church of England are stopped, and freedom of thought and utterance checked within her pale.

Leaving those who are thus represented to deal with this large assertion, we pass on to notice some of the Bishop's answers to his reviewers, who have complained that the Bishop has set forth *nothing new* in his First Part; that his objections had all been heard and answered before. What follows is in Dr. Colenso's words:—"I made, however, no pretence of bringing forward novelties. The very point indeed of my argument in Part I. was this, that these difficulties were *not new*, though many of them were new to me. A great part of this Second Part is liable to the same imputation as the First, as containing no facts which are novelties to those who have already made acquaintance with the subject. But there are portions of the argument, as here stated, in Chapters XII. to XVIII., which, as far as I am aware, are now, for the first time, submitted to the judgment of the learned."

It is quite certain that many of the facts in the First Part are *not new*. It is as certainly the case with the Second, inasmuch as some of the objections in the First Part, and more in the Second, are to be found in Paine's "Age of Reason." We shall quote from that work, placing Paine's writings side by side with Bishop Colenso's words, in order to prove this assertion; and further, we shall refute Bishop Colenso's objections by quoting Bishop Watson's "Apology," addressed to Thomas Paine.

Not new, indeed, as far as the objections go; but surely it is *new* to find a Bishop of the English Church endorsing the opinions of the vilest slanderer of Christianity that ever lived, and putting them forward as his own; indeed, as will be seen, following the "Age of Reason" so closely, as to justify a suspicion that the objections have been taken from that work, and merely deprived of their unbearable blackguardism, to make them presentable.

We certainly confess ourselves unable to see any good reason why these old objections, answered long since, should be raked up from the decent obscurity into which they had passed. Indeed, they seem to us to be brought forward again for the mere purpose of gratifying an ambition for notoriety. If the arguments adduced by Dr. Colenso are not new, if they have been heard, as he admits they have been, and answered, what useful purpose can be served by their revival, or what benefit can they confer upon the Church of Christ in their present form, brought forward by their present sponsor?

The reply our experience furnishes is very saddening; we have reason to believe that Dr. Colenso's work has done mischief he can never repair amongst our brethren of the working classes, by giving rise to an undefined, but wide-spread doubt of the truth and reality of all religion in their minds. There are tens of thousands who will never even see the book itself, whose manner of thought respecting it will be,—that a bishop of the English Church having publicly stated, "the Bible is untruthful," he ought to know best—and consequently they need not, and they will not, trouble themselves further on the subject.

The latest examination into the religious condition of the working classes, brought to light the appalling fact that ninety-eight out of every hundred of their number were living in the habitual neglect of the public worship of God. This census was adopted and repeated by the Earl of Shaftesbury, who publicly stated at the last Annual Meeting of the Preachers of the Open Air Mission that only two per cent. of the working classes attended public worship. We thought the shame and grief of this awful statement hard enough to bear; but now, if our brethren are asked to attend the house of God, their reply will be more disheartening than ever. Surely their religious condition was low enough, without a bishop helping to confirm them in their fatal negligence, their practical atheism in living, as they do, " without God and without hope in the world!"

The next point in the Bishop's preface that we notice, is the remarks he makes concerning an objection in the First Part, which is partially abandoned in the Second. In reference to the priest carrying the bullock, he states:—"The stress of my argument is not laid upon the necessity of the priest himself, in person, doing this; but upon the fact that it *had to be done by somebody*."

This is very cool; these are the words in Part I., p. 40: " *We have to imagine the priest having himself to carry on his back on foot* from St. Paul's to the outskirts of the metropolis, the skin, and flesh, and head, and legs, and inwards, and dung, even the whole bullock."

The Bishop then passes to the consideration of his proposed Substitute for the Bible as it is, by stating:—" Many of my reviewers, as well as some private correspondents, have urged upon me the desirableness of stating at once in what way the usual elements of Christian doctrine appear to be affected by the unhistorical character of the Pentateuch. But, however I may wish to satisfy this very natural impatience, it is impossible to do so till we know what is the residuum of real fact which is left behind when the Pentateuch is thoroughly examined."

As the answer to this question is all that is apparently required, in order to bring out the Bishop's new theory, we are happy in being able, and perfectly willing, to furnish it. How much of the Pentateuch will be left? *The whole of it,* just as it stands at present; for there is little fear of the effect the Bishop's objections will have on the minds of those who will read them thoughtfully. Rather, the effect will be one of absolute relief, displayed as follows: If this is the worst that can be said against the Pentateuch by its proverbially bitterest foe—a friend turned into an enemy—we need not have the slightest fear of the consequences. As we have said, the mischief done will be to those *who will not read* the book, but will take the announced result as sufficiently guaranteed by the character and position of the writer.

But *if the Bishop knows what the new theory is to be,* why can we not have it at once? Let the Bishop assume the credibility of the Pentateuch destroyed (which is unquestionably the only way in which it ever will be), and so bring out to the light the new faith, and let his private correspondents have what their impatient souls are longing for. But this may not be; we are to wait in impatience till—when? It is utterly presumptuous even to think of guessing. In Part I. we were promised Part II.; in Part II. we are promised Part III., which is to consist of a minute criticism of the Book of Genesis. Consequently, with Part III. in possession, we shall apparently be as far off as ever from the promised New Revelation.

We venture, however, to suggest that it might be as well to give some positive idea (however dim it may be in the extreme distance) as to when we may begin to expect it; for if the mouths of cavillers be not thus stopped, they will be apt to suggest that after all there is nothing to give; that it may be well enough for Bishop Colenso to object to the Bible, but that he is too wise in his generation to set up anything of his own, that may fairly be contrasted with what we have now in possession.

In this Second Part of his work the Bishop repeats the assertion, that "the recognition of the gradual growth of Jesus, as the Son of Man, in human knowledge and science of all kind, such as that which concerns the question of the age and authorship of the Pentateuch, is perfectly compatible with, rather is absolutely required by, the most orthodox faith in his divinity as the eternal Son of God."

This is simply repeating the former evasion of the true question at issue, which is—" Had the Lord Jesus absolute and perfect knowledge of who wrote the Pentateuch, or was He ignorant on that subject?" It is distinctly stated that He saw Moses when he, with Elias, appeared on the Mount of Transfiguration. It is evident that they were then personally known to each other, and yet we are to suppose that our Lord was profoundly ignorant of the former life of him who was privileged to talk with Him "of the decease He should accomplish at Jerusalem?" Again, the Bishop talks of our Lord's gradual growth in human knowledge; and we reply that if, even after He rose from the dead, his knowledge was perfected, then it is indisputable that Moses wrote the Pentateuch; for then, after He was risen, "Beginning at Moses and all the prophets, He expounded unto them in all the Scriptures, the things concerning Himself," Luke xxiv. 27.

Why evade or equivocate in a matter of such importance? For the sake of our immortal souls, Christian Minister, if you possess truth that we have not, let us share your advantage; if we are trusting our immortal destiny upon a lie, known and proved, show us how it is so; but beware, oh beware, as you shall stand with us before Christ when He comes to judgment, how you pretend to have knowledge that you have not; how you offend, without full and proved necessity, even one of his little ones, remembering the awful reckoning that must come, when and where there will be neither bishop nor working man.

The Bishop is "naturally most anxious to see what the bishops and doctors of the Church of England will say upon the subject of my book, and how they will act in the present emergency."

He is not, by many thousands, the only one who is waiting and watching for their course of action. We, amongst others, shall be glad to know how far the teaching contained in Parts I. and II. of the Bishop's work, is to be received and recognized by the Heads of the Establishment to which he belongs. We shall be glad to know whether the *dictum*—that pronounces all we have been taught and believe to be most truthful, to be incredible and impossible—will be received by the peers and superiors of the Bishop of Natal in the Church of England. But will the Bishop voluntarily bind himself to abide by their decision? He is pathetic (by anticipation?) upon what *he* calls the "penalties of thought." He tells us they are heavy and hard to bear, instancing the cases of Mr. Heath, who has lost, and paid £9,000; and Mr. Wilson and Dr. Williams, the essayists, who have lost, or may lose, £5,000 more.

But there is certainly another side to this question. If these gentlemen felt themselves aggrieved by the principles or practice of the Church they were connected with, ought they not, as honest men, to have left it, and publicly abandoned all connection with it, before attacking any of the tenets they had sworn to defend?

Following the Bishop in his preface—which appears to include a little of everything—we next find him quoting a passage from the Bishop of London's charge, and passing thence, by easy transition, to Noah's Ark; and he informs us it "was to be furnished by *one* very small window, 'and a window [will the Bishop oblige us with the meaning of the word, rendered window? we have been taught that חַלּוֹן is the Hebrew for window, see Gen. xxvi. 8; while in the account of Noah's Ark the word is צֹהַר]

shalt thou make to the ark, in a cubit (22 inches) shalt thou finish it above;' which window, however, seems never to have been opened till the end of the deluge, if indeed it could have been opened during the fall of rain; in which case, as they had no glass in those days, the inmates of the ark could have had neither light nor air."

What are we to say to writing like this? It is better to own the truth at once, we think the Bishop is making fun of us! It is quite impossible he can be writing seriously, for if he is, he must certainly estimate the intellect of the readers of his work as low as it is possible to do. But if this is not ridicule with a grave face, we will ask—Did the Bishop ever see the plates to Calmet? If not, we will inform him that he will there find *suggested*, that although the window might be only twenty-two inches high, yet that it was possible to carry it *at that height* all round the ark, both sides and ends, and the projecting roof over the opening might be a sufficient protection from the rain of the deluge, even though it were open day and night.

The Bishop thus continues: " I assert, however, without fear of contradiction, that there are multitudes now of the more intelligent clergy who do not believe in the reality of the Noachian deluge, as described in the Book of Genesis. Yet did ever a layman hear his clergyman speak out distinctly what he thought, and say plainly from the pulpit what he himself believed, and what he would have them believe on this point? . . . Have not your clergy *kept back* from you their thoughts hitherto, not only about the deluge, but about a multitude of other matters such as those treated of in Part I. of this book? Let the laity answer the above questions for themselves."

We will endeavour to answer; and would therefore ask: Does the Bishop take Englishmen in 1863 for Zulus? Does he think for a moment we are dependent *on our clergy* for our geological knowledge? or that they *could*, even if they *would*, keep back geological or any other knowledge from us? Did the Bishop of Natal ever hear of " Cassell's Popular Educator," in penny numbers, circulated by hundreds of thousands? Does he know that in that publication there are articles written by a Clergyman, or Dissenting minister (we do not know or care which just now), embracing the whole science of Geology? Did he never hear of Dr. Hitchcock's "Religion of Geology," price 1*s*. 6*d*., or of "The Course of Creation," by Rev. John Anderson, or of Dr. Buckland's works, or of "The Pre-Adamite Earth" of Dr. Harris? Evidently the Bishop of Natal has been so long amongst the Zulus that he is totally ignorant of the position even of working men at home. We will help him by informing him that the most spirited discussion we have heard for some time took place in our Working Men's Discussion Class on the subject: "Was the deluge partial or universal?" and that it occupied us for three evenings in succession.

But there is something deeper here. It is evident that the Bishop does not believe in the fact of the deluge. We beg to ask him why he does not? Will he show us that Geology must necessarily take cognizance of such a temporary matter as one year's flood must have been, geologically speaking? Will he point out to us any nation on the face of the earth, whose *traditions* date back anywhere near the time specified, where the tradition of a deluge is not found? Will he prove that these *universal traditions* have no foundation in fact; or will he, for instance, prove to us the falsehood of Dr. Pye Smith's theory of the Noachian deluge? It is easy to sneer, easier to treat such a subject with assumed contempt; but we may surely ask for proof of its being a myth, before we cease to believe in the reality of the Noachian deluge; and there is not one word of such proof at present published by the Bishop of Natal.

Our preface is already too long, and we must therefore pass over some matters we would willingly notice; such as the Bishop's promise to submit himself to the judgment of the Church when proved to be wrong—in his own judgment of himself—a safe promise! The Bishop concludes his preface with an extract from HENGSTENBERG, as follows:—" The author thinks he has a right to expect that, as he has employed arguments in this book, he will be answered with arguments. If this righteous demand should not be acceded to the loss will not fall upon him, but on those who attempt to annihilate evidence with abuse."

Should not a man come into court with clean hands? If so, surely the Bishop does not. These are some of his words: " Let, then, my Right Reverend Brother, who has judged and condemned me, answer my arguments by a book . . . and not seek to put them down by sneers, by mere declamation from the pulpit or platform, or by sending a brief of excommunication to the *Times*." The Bishop charges the whole body of the Church of England Clergy (*as such*) with having deliberately, and of set purpose kept back the truth they knew from their congregations. He stigmatizes them also as follows—"I am saddened and humiliated, I blush with shame for the Church of England." Surely no body of men were ever in a better position to return the compliment. Again he individualizes in imagination—" Is it not because the clergy, bound by their ordination vows, *dare not 'think'* at all on such subjects, or, if they do, *dare not express freely their thoughts* from the pulpit, or by means of the press, without incurring the awful charge of 'heresy,' and the danger of being dragged into the Ecclesiastical Court by some clerical brother who has himself *no turn, perhaps no faculty, for thinking*, or who has else *abandoned his rights and duties as a reasoning man* to become *the mere exponent of a church-system* or a creed, but who will, at least, *prevent others from exercising their powers of thought* in the inquiry after truth, and so disturbing the quiet repose of the Church."

No abuse or wholesale misrepresentation here, of course! And once more, the Bishop says of his brother clergymen—"*Some good, easy brother who never, perhaps, knew what it was to have a passionate yearning for the truth as truth,* who never made a sacrifice in the search, or for the maintenance of it, and *never, in fact, gave himself an hour's hard 'thinking' in his life.*"

After these specimens of courtesy of language, we think the man must be a proficient in abuse who can produce any thing more unprovoked, uncalled for, and wantonly insulting.

But the Bishop has indisputably exercised *his* "powers of thought," and that with a most disastrous effect upon his reputation. The utter folly of the conclusion to which he comes, the effective manner in which he demonstrates the truth of his own theory to be impossible, we have set forth in Chapter XX. There the reader will find Bishop Colenso asserting that there are no Jehovistic names in the early chapters of Samuel, and *then quoting a Jehovistic name from the very first verse in the book.* He also gravely states his belief that Samuel first formed and invented the name Jehovah, *after* he has demonstrated that to have invented the name, Samuel must have invented the name of *his own great grandfather, Elihu.*

The whole of this Second Part is founded upon the assumption that Samuel was the Elohist, and invented the name Jehovah, notwithstanding this name was, according to *Dr. Colenso's own showing*, in use at least four generations before Samuel was born.

How Bishop Colenso could fall into such a ridiculous error, and one of such magnitude as to ruin his whole theory, is, to us, inconceivable; but that he has so erred is indisputable. Throughout his work, he again and again repeats his theory concerning Samuel's authorship, and his first forming and inventing the name

B

Jehovah—commencing by putting the case as a probability, he advances by larger strides, though still doubtingly, until near the end of the book, where Samuel's invention of the name of Jehovah is boldly and repeatedly asserted.

And Bishop Colenso is evidently quite unconscious that the name of Elihu, *quoted by himself*, is utterly ruinous to his case. Indeed, he quotes the first part of this name, *El*—God—to prove the Elohistic names in the First Book of Samuel, but he does not see that the last part consists of a contracted form of the name Jehovah, which he has pointed out in Chap. XIX.

In one sentence of about two lines, Bishop Colenso says:— " Here, throughout the first chapter, we do not meet with a single name compounded with Jehovah, though we find *El*kanah and *El*ihu."

But this name, Elihu, interpreted, is God-Jehovah, and it proves that the name (Jehovah) asserted to have been invented by Samuel, had been known in his family at least a century before he was born.

We need add nothing to this exposure; it has only to be made known to deprive Dr. Colenso of all claim to be regarded as an authority in matters of criticism.

We add a few words concerning ourselves. In this Second Part we shall somewhat widen our plan; and while keeping ourselves solely to the subjects chosen by the Bishop, we shall endeavour to set forth some small portion of the affirmative evidence of Scripture Inspiration. It has been pointed out to us that in our anxiety to do justice to the Bishop, we have been wanting in duty to our own cause, in neglecting to show, as occasion served, the strength of the position of the believer.

But when stating the Bishop's objections we shall, as before, always quote them in his own words.

"CHAPTER I.

SIGNS OF DIFFERENT AUTHORS IN THE PENTATEUCH."

Such is the heading affixed by Bishop Colenso to the first chapter of his Second Part. The chapter consists of twelve pages; eight of the twelve are taken up with repetitions of former objections; here, the Bishop refers again to the number of warriors being 600,000, and further shows that the figures are correct as they stand. We perfectly agree with him in this matter, thinking that it is impossible to touch these figures, which turn up so often and in such various ways, without destroying the credibility of the Narrative. We do not see any reason why they should be altered, nor has any valid reason for alteration been shown in the Bishop's book, or in any comment upon it that we have seen. The Bishop then passes on to reply to his Reviewers respecting the lack of firewood, water, and grass in the Wilderness; but merely reiterates what he has said before, and we have answered; and we may therefore proceed to the subject of the chapter, which is thus stated by the Bishop:—

"Now, however, that we are able to feel that we stand on sure ground, when we assert that these books, whatever be their value, with whatever pious purpose they were written, and whatever excellent lessons they may teach, are not removed from the sphere of critical inquiry, by possessing any such Divine infallibility as has been usually ascribed to them, there is a multitude of other difficulties, inconsistencies, and impossibilities, which will be at once apparent, if we examine carefully the Scripture narrative, and no longer suffer our eyes to be blinded, by the mere force of habit, to the actual meaning of the words which we read. Without, at present, stopping to consider those which arise from examining the story of the Creation and the Fall, as given in the first chapters of Genesis, by the light of modern science, we will here notice the contradictions which exist between the first account of the creation in Gen. i. 1,—ii. 3, and the second account in Gen. ii. 4—25. . . . . . The following are the most noticeable points of difference between the two cosmogonies.

" (I.) In the first, the earth emerges from the waters, and is, therefore, saturated with moisture, i. 9, 10.

"In the second the 'whole face of the ground' requires to be moistened, ii. 6."

This is the first difficulty we are to examine, and it will not occupy much time. It is not said in the Narrative in chap. i. that the new earth *was saturated* with moisture. The Bishop has tacked on that supposition in order to create his difficulty; and it is not said in chap. ii. that the whole face of the ground *required* to be moistened; this circumstance, also, the Bishop has supposed and thrust into the Narrative, in order to complete the statement of the difficulty; which is of his own invention from first to last. These are the two statements run into one :—"And God said, Let the waters under the heaven be gathered together unto one place, and let the dry land appear, and it was so. And God called the dry land, earth, and the gathering together of the waters called He seas; and God saw that it was good; . . . But there went up a mist from the earth and watered the whole face of the ground."

We need only notice that the Narrative says expressly, that the land was *dry*, and the Bishop's theory makes it necessary for him to say it was *saturated with moisture*. Doubtless the *surface* of the newly emerged earth was wet, but if upheaved by volcanic agency accompanied by the emission of intense heat from the interior, it would not be long before mist or rain would be needed.

"(II.) In the first, the birds and beasts are created before man, i. 20, 24, 26.

"In the second, man is created before the birds and beasts, ii. 7, 19."

It is stated that man was the last creation in the first chapter of Genesis, and all the records of geology yet known and verified confirm the truth of the statement. Any geologist will readily affirm from his science, that the last appearances are those of the human frame, and the work of the human hands. The Bishop has not yet asserted the contrary, and therefore we may take it for granted. In the second chapter, there is no statement of the *time* or order of the creation of bird, or beast, or man. The fact of the creation mentioned in chapter i. as regards birds and beasts is reiterated in chapter ii., and this further information is given, that they were brought to Adam to be named. By reading the two passages it will be clearly seen that there is no contradiction or even discrepancy.

"(III.) In the first 'all fowls that fly' are made out of the *waters*, i. 20.

"In the second the fowls of the air are made out of the *ground*, ii. 19."

This trashy objection is founded upon a word *expressly marked, as added by the translators* in the English version. Take away the added word, and the objection instantly disappears. There is also in the margin of the English Bible the true translation of the Hebrew, and when thus corrected and read, the verse does not state from whence the fowls were created. We subjoin the corrected verse, Gen. i. 20—"And God said, Let the waters bring forth abundantly the moving creature that hath life. And let fowl fly in the open firmament of heaven." To prove our case we subjoin the verse taken from the Hebrew Reading Lessons, published by Bagster, with the literal translation beneath it.

הַמָּיִם	יִשְׁרְצוּ	אֱלֹהִים	וַיֹּאמֶר
waters-the	abundantly-forth-bring-Let	, God	said-And

הָאָרֶץ עַל־	יְעוֹפֵף וְעוֹף	חַיָּה נֶפֶשׁ	שֶׁרֶץ
earth-the upon	fly-let fowl-and	; life of soul	, things-creeping

הַשָּׁמָיִם׃	רְקִיעַ	פְּנֵי	עַל־
.heaven-the	of-expanse-the	of-face-the	upon

We ask if there is here a single word stating that the fowls were created out of the *waters*, as the Bishop has asserted. That they were created from the ground was no doubt true; are not both man and beast thus created in our time out of the ground? though, it may be, through the *via media* of ordinary parentage; and if thus still created out of the ground and sustained solely from it, then the announcement that man was created out of the ground, "Dust thou art, and unto dust shalt thou return," is not "unhistorical," but historically, physiologically, and literally true. And this is the testimony of science, not against, but in favour of the Bible.

" (IV.) In the first, man is created in the image of God, i. 27.

"In the second, man is made of the dust of the ground, and merely animated with the breath of life, and it is only after his eating the forbidden fruit that the LORD God said, 'Behold the man has become as one of us, to know good and evil,' ii. 7; iii. 22."

The general statement of the creation of the human race on the sixth day is made in i. 27. How they were created is not mentioned; the broad general facts of creation in the image of

God, distinction of sex, of God's blessing and man's sovereignty, are distinctly stated, but nothing more. In the second the *modus operandi* of man's creation is revealed: the accounts are complementary not contradictory, and some time afterward (as we think in great mercy), the fallen and therefore miserable man is prevented from perpetuating his misery by taking an immortality of sin and sorrow upon himself. There is no contradiction throughout; the word *merely* on which the Bishop's objection rests, is introduced by him, to make the objection, which exists in *his statement of the case* only; it is not found in the Narrative.

"(V.) In the first, the man is made the lord of the whole earth, i. 28.

"In the second, he is merely placed in the garden of Eden to dress it and to keep it, ii. 8, 15."

The first is the commission given to Adam as the representative of his race, the second is the commencement of his individual history, as any intelligent Sunday-school scholar could inform the Bishop; the same word—*merely*—is here again introduced to make the objection.

"(VI.) In the first, man and woman are created *together*, as the closing and completing work of the whole creation, created also, as is evidently implied, in the same kind of way, to be the complement of one another; and, thus created, they are blessed together, i. 28.

"In the second, the beasts and birds are created *between* the man and the woman. First, the man is made of the dust of the ground, he is placed by himself in the garden, charged with a solemn command, and threatened with a curse if he breaks it, then the beasts and the birds are made, and the man gives names to them; and, lastly, after all this, the woman is made out of one of his ribs, but merely as a helpmate for the man, ii. 7, 8, 15, 22."

It will be seen by reading the texts that the statement "created *together*" italicised by the Bishop above, is *merely* an addition of his own to make his point; if it were in the Narrative it would be a different matter. We have shown that the birds and beasts were not created *between* the man and the woman, as the *time* of their creation is not stated in chapter ii. at all, and we do not think there is anything else here needing notice.

We now pause to point out that from such utter nonsense as these six *manufactured* objections exhibit, through the results arrived at by such unscrupulous dealing with the Holy Scriptures, we are to be brought to doubt the knowledge and the wisdom of the Lord of glory. Well may Bishop Colenso shrink, as he does, from publishing his ideas as concerning the Lord Jesus Christ, for what must be *the end* of that theory, which in *its very commencement* finds degrading insinuations concerning our Lord's knowledge absolutely necessary?

"CHAPTER II.
THE ELOHISTIC AND JEHOVISTIC WRITERS."

WE take the first statement from the end of chapter I. of the Bishop's book, where he has thus written:—" The fact is that the *second* account of the creation (ii. 4—25), together with the story of the Fall (iii.), is manifestly composed by a different writer altogether from him who wrote the *first* (i. 1,—ii. 3).

This is suggested at once by the circumstance that, throughout the first narrative, the Creator is always spoken of by the name אֱלֹהִים ELOHIM, GOD; whereas throughout the second account, as well as the story of the Fall, He is always called יְהוָֹה אֱלֹהִים JEHOVAH ELOHIM, LORD GOD, except in iii. 1, 3, 5, where the writer seems to abstain, for some reason, from placing the name 'Jehovah' in the mouth of the serpent. This accounts naturally for the above contradictions. It would appear that, for some reason, the productions of two pens have been here united, without reference to their inconsistencies."

And the Bishop continues in Chapter II.:—" One of these two writers, it will be found, is distinguished by the *constant* use of the word Elohim; the other by the intermixture with it of the word Jehovah, which two words appear in the English Version as God and Lord. Hence these two parts of the book are generally known as the Elohistic and Jehovistic portions. The Jehovistic passages taken by themselves are mere disjointed fragments, and require the Elohistic story to connect them with each other. This implies at once that the Elohist was the oldest of the two writers, and that his narrative may have been used by the other, as the *groundwork* upon which he framed his own additions. The Jehovist, in fact, may have revised what the Elohist had written, making his own insertions here and there, sometimes in long passages (as in the second account of the creation), sometimes in shorter ones (as in the small section about the Deluge), sometimes interpolating two or three verses only, or even a single verse or part of a verse, which makes its appearance in the midst of the older writings, and now and then in such a way as to make it difficult to assign precisely to each writer his own particular portion. In most cases, however, the distinction of the two hands is so plain that it cannot be mistaken by any attentive reader. But this circumstance, viz., that such unmistakeable differences of expression distinguish, throughout the book of Genesis, the parts which are due to these separate writers, may, almost, with reference to the momentous questions involved, be called providential, since it enables us to speak positively on some points, which might otherwise have been still subject to doubt, and will be found greatly to relieve the difficulty of determining, with some approach to probability, the age of the different portions of the Pentateuch."

There is a confident coolness of assertion throughout this

quotation that is almost enough to make any one (not accustomed to Dr. Colenso) believe it; but we think it will come upon many educated Englishmen with something like surprise. Where are our English works on this subject? What English scholars have added to the development of this new theory? Who amongst those we know and respect have given in their adhesion to it? What books by English authors have been published on this subject? The answer is very simple; we do not know of a single English author who has written and published any work specially devoted to this interesting subject. There may be such, but we can assert that all our time is passed amongst printing and bookbinding, and we have not heard of a single one.

As far as we know, the whole question is almost exclusively confined to German authors; but some of their works have been translated into English, and the result is not quite a mystery. But if one-hundredth part of the Bishop's large assertions be truthful, there must be some recognized standard adopted by Elohistic and Jehovistic writers; some one amongst the German writers on this subject who, having mastered it in all its details, is looked up to by other writers as an authority? The answer to this question is an exposure of the utter hollowness of the Bishop's theory, and of the audacity of his method of writing; but as an infinitely more competent hand than ours has dealt with this subject—has exposed the Bishop's argument *by anticipation* in a way to make any one laugh that will compare the crushing exposure, *published before the theory*, with the Bishop's statement; we shall venture to show the real position of this question, as it is stated by a clergyman, who both Jews and Christians unite in affirming to be one of the best living Hebrew scholars—Dr. A. McCaul writing in "Aids to Faith."

"To discuss all the details of criticism would require volumes, but one alleged result, often stated in an off-hand, popular way—

asserted with unhesitating confidence, and repeated as absolutely certain, requires notice. It is said that in the book of Genesis there are some portions in which God is spoken of exclusively as Elohim—in others exclusively as Jehovah [the LORD in the authorized version]. This exclusive use of the one Divine name in some portions, and of the other in other portions, it is said, characterizes two different authors living at different times; and, consequently, Genesis is composed of two different documents, the one Elohistic, the other Jehovistic, which, moreover, differ in statement; and, consequently, that this book was not written by Moses, and is neither inspired nor trustworthy.

"Now, let us look at this statement as a supposed result of criticism. It is generally urged as if on this point critics were all of one mind, agreed in the portions which are Elohistic or Jehovistic—unanimous as to the characteristic differences of style in the separate portion; in fact, as if the theory came with universal consent. [Did Dr. McCaul know what Bishop Colenso intended to write and publish, and anticipate it?] This is not the case in the present theory; the popular statement given above does not represent the true state of the case,—the fact is, that there is here the greatest variety of opinion, and the modifications of the above apparently simple theory are so widely divergent as either to shake the value of the criticism, *or throw a dark shade of doubt on the competence of the critics.*

"In the first place, there is a difference as to the extent to which the theory is to be applied. Some confine it to the book of Genesis, others include Exodus to chapter vi.; others, as Knobel, Bleek, and Ewald, assert, that the Jehovistic and Elohistic differences can be recognized through the whole Pentateuch to the end of Joshua. Some, as J. D. Michaelis, Jahn, Vater, Hartmann, regard Genesis as a loose and unsystematic stringing together of disjointed fragments. But passing these by, let us look at the state of the Elohistic and Jehovistic theory as stated by Bleek in his Introduction.

"In the year 1753 Astruc, a French physician, taught that the book of Genesis is made up of twelve memoirs or documents, of which the two principal are the Elohistic and the Jehovistic.

"Eichhorn asserted that the present book of Genesis is based upon two pre-Mosaic documents, distinguished by Elohim and Jehovah. . . . . . Sometimes the accounts are mixed together. Some other documents were consulted.

"Ilgen supposes seventeen documents, but only three authors, one Jehovist, two Elohists; and is so acute in his scent as sometimes to divide even single verses between the three, and give to each his own.

"De Wette's theory in the first edition of his Introduction is, that a continuous Elohistic document pervades and forms the basis of the whole book, and extends to Exodus vi. In this the author inserted what he found in one; or, probably, in several Jehovistic documents.

"Von Bohlen believes in the same Elohistic basis, but denies the existence of Jehovistic documents. The author of the book in its present state is the Jehovist, so that only two persons are concerned.

"Gramberg makes three authors—the Elohist, the Jehovist, and the compiler, who does not scruple sometimes to substitute one divine name for the other.

"Ewald exhibits a variety of opinions; he began by holding the unity of Genesis, and proving it against both the document and the fragment hypothesis. His arguments have not yet been refuted either by himself or others. . . . . He ascribes Genesis in its present form to that writer whom, in his first edition, he calls the fourth narrator, and, in his second edition, the fifth narrator of the primitive histories, who lived in the time of Jotham. This work had several predecessors, according to the first edition, three; according to the second, six. Three of these are Elohistic.

"Hupfeldt takes as the basis of our Genesis three independent historic works—two Elohistic, one Jehovistic, and makes in addition a compiler.

"Knobel believes in two documents—first, the Elohistic, forming the basis of the Pentateuch and of Joshua; second, the Jehovistic; which again has two previous sources. There are, besides, free Jehovistic developments, in which the compiler sometimes followed hints in the two documents, sometimes popular tradition, and sometimes his own conceptions."

This enumeration is far from exhausting the varieties, but it is sufficient to show the want of unity. The reader will perceive that some assert one Elohistic document; others two; others three. In like manner, some make one Jehovist, some more. Some make the Jehovist identical with the compiler; others make him a different person. Some make two, others three, others four, Ewald seven documents by different authors, the materials of Genesis. . . . . And thus the most celebrated critics convict each other of false criticism. Hupfeldt condemns Knobel; Ewald condemns Hupfeldt and Knobel; Knobel condemns Ewald and Hupfeldt. If Knobel's criticism is correct, Hupfeldt is worthless. If Ewald be right, the others must be deficient in critical acumen. They may all be wrong, but only one of the three can be right.

"But take into the account all the other differences enumerated above, one supposing that the documents are pre-Mosaic, another that they were written in the times of Joshua or the Judges; another in the time of David [this is the theory adopted by Bishop Colenso]; another some centuries later; and how uncertain must the principles of their criticism appear; how valueless their conclusions! With such facts, can any sane person talk of the results of modern criticism as regards the Book of Genesis? or be willing to give up the belief of centuries for such criticism as this?

"It is self-evident that criticism leading to such inconsistent conclusions must be in a high degree imaginative. A little examination shows that it is also unreasonably arbitrary. In order to make out the theory that there are two authors, one of whom is known by the exclusive use of Elohim, and the other by the exclusive use of Jehovah, and that the former is more ancient than the latter, it is necessary to point out paragraphs in which those divine names are exclusively used, and also to prove that the Elohist does not refer to the Jehovistic document, for if the Elohist plainly refers to what the Jehovist has related, the latter cannot be posterior to the former, and the theory fails. Now, unhappily for the theory, the word Jehovah does occur in the Elohistic passages, and the Elohist does refer to the Jehovistic narrative. Thus, in Gen. xi. 4, the two names occur together—'These are the generations of the heavens and the earth when they were created, in the day when Jehovah Elohim made the earth and the heavens.' Now, if this verse belongs to what precedes, then the following narrative, which has also the unusual union of the two names, was written by the Elohist, and the first three chapters are by one author. If it be written by the Jehovist, how comes it to have Elohim as well, and why does it differ both from Elohist and Jehovist documents by the union of the names? Here is a difficulty which has divided all Germany, and arrayed Rationalist against Rationalist, and Orthodox against Orthodox, and for which there seems no hope of solution, unless violence be offered to the text, and men be persuaded against the evidence of manuscripts and ancient versions, that the words, 'These are the generations of the heaven and the earth,' stood originally as the heading before the first verse of the first chapter, and that the word Elohim, in ii. 4, is an interpolation of the Jehovist. Take another example. Genesis v. is said to be Elohistic, and it is certain that *Elohim*, God, occurs five times, but in verse 29 appears the word *Jehovah* to disturb the theorist; and not only is this word there, but the verse refers to the Jehovistic chapter iii. 17. What is to be done? The verse stands in all the manuscripts and ancient versions. But if the Elohistic theory is to stand, it must be got rid of somehow. It is an interpolation, says the theorist; it was put in by the compiler. In like manner, the theorists cut off chapter vii. 9—24, from its context, and say, it is Elohistic. But, lo! in verse 16 stands 'Jehovah.' The same canon of the old Socinian criticism is again applied; the unwelcome word is an interpolation. One instance more. The forty-ninth chapter is said to belong to a long Elohistic portion. But in the 18th verse occur these words of Jacob, 'I have waited for thy salvation, O Jehovah.' Again the same violence is repeated. The disturbing verse is an interpolation. Is this criticism? Is it a fair and legitimate proceeding to alter the text, and that not once but frequently, in order to make it suit one's theory?—to discard the consent of manuscripts, ancient versions, all printed editions, and cry out, 'Interpolation! Interpolation!' without any authority at all? There is no more certain sign of helpless prejudice, or critical incompetence, than to have frequent resource to violent and unauthorized alteration of the text; and yet, without this, the theory of the Elohistic and Jehovistic documents, even if it were unanimously received by modern critics, could not be made out. Arbitrary separations of what evidently belongs together, and unwarranted assertions of interpolation, prove its unsoundness. The variety of its modifications, one neutralizing the other, as has been shown above, demonstrates the uncertainty and untrustworthiness of the results."

It would be altogether out of place for us to add a single

word to this annihilating exposure of the theory Bishop Colenso has adopted. It is certain that the Bishop has seen it, inasmuch as he makes a quotation from the very same page whence the conclusion of our extract is taken. The only wonder is that after seeing it, he should think of foisting the conclusions of such critics upon men who have read Dr. McCaul's Essay.

That Bishop Colenso feels acutely the great strength of Dr. McCaul's position is evident, from the following extract from the Bishop's writing:—" Gen. xvii. 1. ' The LORD appeared to Abraham, and said unto him, I am the Almighty God.' " And he adds in a foot-note, " The occurrence of the name Jehovah in this verse (N.B., *in this verse only* of the whole chapter) will be considered when we review the whole book of Genesis in Part III."

Why not enter into it where it is most needed? Why leave or evade the consideration of an utterly destructive verse to an indefinite period? Until we get the explanation, we must hold the Bishop's Elohistic theory entirely unproven, even upon his own showing.

"CHAPTER III.

THE EARLIER HISTORICAL BOOKS OF THE OLD TESTAMENT."

THE Bishop says: "We must next endeavour to arrive at some clearer notion, from an examination of the Books of the Pentateuch themselves, as to the time when, the persons by whom, and the circumstances under which, they were most probably written. Here, first, it should be noticed that the Books of the Pentateuch are never ascribed to Moses in the inscriptions of Hebrew manuscripts, or in printed copies of the Hebrew Bible. Nor are they styled the Books of Moses in the Septuagint or Vulgate, but only in our modern translations, after the example of many eminent fathers of the Church, who, with the exception of JEROME, and, perhaps,

ORIGEN, were one and all of them very little acquainted with the Hebrew language, and still less with its criticism."

This is a choice specimen, either of gross ignorance or of the most disgraceful quibbling. We are to notice that "the Books of the Pentateuch are never ascribed to Moses in the inscriptions of Hebrew manuscripts, or in printed copies of the Hebrew Bible." We admit this, but they are ascribed to him, in a place of far higher authority, that is, *in the text itself*, as follows:—
"When Moses had made an end of writing the words of this law in a book until they were finished, ... Moses commanded the Levites which bare the ark of the covenant of the Lord, saying, Take this book of the law, and put it in the side of the ark of the covenant of the LORD your God, that it may be there for a witness against thee," Deut. xxxi. 24—26. Here, in the original, the identical words are inserted סֵפֶר הַתּוֹרָה (book of the law), which has been the Hebrew name of the Pentateuch from the time of Moses to the present day.

There is nothing in this chapter that needs any further remark. There are no objections stated; and if the chapter has any meaning at all, it must be in connection with arguments in more advanced chapters in the Book.

"CHAPTER IV.

THE LATER HISTORICAL BOOKS OF THE OLD TESTAMENT."

THIS chapter contains an analytical account of the Books of Chronicles, Ezra, and Nehemiah; and enters into some genealogical questions to be found therein; but as these questions lie far apart from the main subject, the Pentateuch, we shall pass them over. Indeed, we have failed to discover the intention of Dr.

Colenso in writing these Chapters III. and IV. For all practical purposes they might as well have been omitted; their only use being, as far as we can see, to make up the book. There is, however, a specimen, at the end of Chapter IV., of the Bishop's mode of argument that may be worth pointing out. Dr. Colenso states:—"In 1 Chron. xxix. 7, we find the Persian coin, daric, referred to familiarly, as if it had been long in use among the Jews. This coin, however, could not have been freely employed among the Jews till some time after its first introduction, which *is supposed* to have been in the reign of Darius Hystaspes, B.C. 521—486. It appears, therefore, that these Jews must have been for some time under Persian government before these books could have been written."

It will be seen that the large assertion which closes the quotation is founded solely upon the *supposed*, not the known date of a Persian coin. Again, the Bishop writes: "The Book of Esther refers to events in the reign of Ahasuerus, *supposed* by some to have been the same Artaxerxes by whom Ezra was sent to Jerusalem, but more *probably* his father Xerxes, who reigned in Persia from B.C. 486 to B.C. 465; from which we see the earliest date at which this book could have been written."

It will be noticed that the Bishop settles this question upon the authorities of a *supposition*, and a *probability* which contradict each other: but he does not venture to assert the truth of either one or the other, though founding his argument upon them; nor does he assign any reason why we should not reject both. To attempt to refute arguments *confessedly founded upon* "*it is supposed*" and "*more probably*" is mere waste of time.

"CHAPTERS V. AND VI.

SIGNS OF LATER DATE IN THE PENTATEUCH."

THE Bishop writes thus:—"Returning now to the consideration of the Pentateuch, we have already seen reason to conclude that the account of the Exodus generally, as there narrated, could not have been written by Moses, or by any one of his contemporaries. The following instances will tend still further to confirm the above conclusion, by showing, as we might expect, that the Pentateuch as a whole, taking with it also the book of Joshua, was written at a much later date than the age of Moses and the Exodus."

Reading over these "signs of later date," we instantly recognized many of them as old acquaintances at Infidel Lectures, and the thought came into our minds, surely the greater part of these are taken, without acknowledgment, from Tom Paine's "Age of Reason." Determined to verify our thoughts, we procured a copy of that delectable work, edited and published by Holyoake, in Fleet Street, and occupied half-an-hour in comparing Dr. Colenso's "Critical Examination of the Pentateuch" with Thomas Paine's "Age of Reason." We now place the result of our comparison before our readers. It next occurred to us, that if the objections were found in Paine's work, the replies thereunto would appear in Bishop Watson's "Apology for Religion," written in reply, and personally addressed to Paine. Finding this to be the case, that Bishop Watson's arguments, addressed to Paine, the Infidel, were equally available in refutation of his "Right Reverend Brother" the Bishop of Natal, we have appended Bishop Watson's answers to both the assailants of the Bible, the Infidel (*seniores priores*) and the Bishop, who are, indisputably, fitting companions for each other.

PAINE'S "AGE OF REASON."	BISHOP COLENSO'S "EXAMINATION."
"'And that he pursued them unto Dan, ver. 14.' There was no such place as Dan till many years after the death of Moses, and consequently that Moses could not be the writer of the Book of Genesis where this account of pursuing them unto *Dan* is given." (P. 38.)	"'And pursued them unto Dan, Gen. xiv. 14.' But the place was not named Dan till long after the death of Moses; for we read, Josh. xix. 47, 'Dan went up to fight against Leshem, and took it, and smote it with the edge of the sword, and possessed it, and dwelt therein, *and called Leshem, Dan, after the name of Dan, their father.*" (P. 201.)

"I desire it may be proved that the DAN mentioned in Genesis was the same town as Dan mentioned in Judges. I desire further to have it proved that the Dan mentioned in Genesis was the name of a town, and not of a river. It is merely said that Abraham pursued them to Dan. Now a river was full as likely as a town to stop a pursuit. Lot we know was settled in the plain of Jordan, and Jordan, we know, was composed of the united streams of two rivers, Jor and Dan." (Watson, p. 29.)

| "The passage, therefore, that these are the kings that reigned in the land of Edom before there reigned *any* king over the children of Israel, could only have been written after the first king began to reign over them, and consequently the Book of Genesis, so far from having been written by Moses, could not | "'And these are the kings that reigned in the land of Edom before there reigned *any* king over the children of Israel,' Gen. xxxvi. 31. The phrase 'before there reigned any king over the children of Israel' is here used in such a way as to imply that *one* king at least had reigned, or was reigning, over the chil- |

have been written till the time of Saul at least, and if taken in a general sense, it carries itself through all the times of the Jewish monarchy." (P. 39.)

dren of Israel; that is, apparently, not over one of the separate kingdoms of Judah or Israel, but over the united people; in other words, it could not have been written *before* the time of Samuel." (P. 202.)

"A small addition to a book does not destroy either the genuineness or the authenticity of the whole book. I am not ignorant of the manner in which commentators have answered this objection of Spinoza. . . . . Interpolations have happened to other books, but these interpolations by other hands have never been considered as invalidating the authority of those books." (Watson, p. 29.)

We do not see any necessity to consider this passage an interpolation. Moses is here simply relating the fulfilment of the first part of the prediction to Sarah, that "kings of people shall be of her," Gen. xvii. 16. Moses knew from acquaintance with the prophecy that kings should eventually reign over Israel, and he therefore speaks of the fact as certain of accomplishment concerning the Israelites. And by thus pointing out kings from Esau, and thereby bringing the accomplishment of the prediction, concerning these descendants of Sarah, to the minds of the children of Jacob; Moses was enabled to appease a people so mistrustful and discontented as that which he brought up from Egypt, and to assure them that they also should ultimately be under royal government in their own promised land.

"This tale of the sun standing still upon Mount Gibeon, and the moon in the valley of

"'And the sun stood still, and the moon stayed, until the people had avenged themselves

Ajalon, is one of those fables that detects itself."

" Such a circumstance could not have happened without being known all over the world, whereas there is not a nation in the world that knows anything about it. But why must the moon stand still ? What occasion could there be for moonlight in the daytime, and that too whilst the sun shined? The account shows the ignorance of Joshua, for he should have commanded the earth to have stood still."

upon their enemies. Is not this written in the book of Jasher ?'" (Josh. x. 13.)

"It is inconceivable that if Joshua really wrote this book he should have referred, for the details of such an extraordinary miracle in which he himself was primarily concerned, to another book as the book of Jasher" (p. 205). "The arresting of the earth's motion, while it might cause the appearance of the sun standing still, would not account for the moon staying." (Preface, Part I., p. 11.)

" You are probably mistaken as to the fact of this miracle being unknown; a confused tradition concerning this miracle, and a similar one in the time of Ahaz is reported in Beloe's Herodotus. . . . . The machine of the universe is in the hands of God; He can stop the motion of any part of it, or of the whole of it, with less trouble and less danger of injuring it than you can stop your watch. In testimony of the reality of the miracle, the author of the book says, Is not this written in the Book of Jasher? No author in his senses would have appealed in proof of his veracity to a book that did not exist." (Watson, p. 38.)

" The writer lived long after the time of Moses, as is evident from the expression, ' unto this day.'"

" The frequent occurrence of the expression, ' unto this day.' 'No man knoweth of his [Moses'] sepulchre unto this day.' Deu. xxxiv. 6." (p. 209.)

"A distant, but general term is also expressed in the eighth chapter: 'And Joshua burnt Ai, and made it an heap for ever, even a desolation *unto this day.*'" (P. 43.)

"'And Joshua burnt Ai, and made it an heap for ever, even a desolation *unto this day.*' Josh. viii. 28." (P. 209.)

"Joshua lived twenty-four years after the burning of Ai, and if he wrote his history in the latter part of his life, what absurdity is there in saying, Ai is in ruins, to this very day?" (Watson, p. 39.) It is also well known to every Jew, and every Hebrew Bible shows it, that the Hebrew Torah (Pentateuch) originally ended with Deut. xxxi.; and if Joshua wrote the last chapter of Deuteronomy, there could be no difficulty in believing that he said, "No man knoweth of his sepulchre 'unto this day.'"

"The length of the bed was 16 feet 4 inches, and the breadth 7 feet 4 inches. The writer says, Is it not in Rabbath, of the children of Ammon?"

"For only Og, King of Bashan, remained of the remnants of the giants; behold his bedstead was a bedstead of iron. Is it not in Rabbath of the children of Ammon? nine cubits (16½ feet) was the length thereof, and four cubits (7¼ feet) the breadth of it."

"But it could not be Moses that said this, because Moses could know nothing about Rabbah nor of what was in it. The knowledge, therefore, that this bed was at Rabbah and of the particulars of its dimensions must be referred to the time

"But only a very short time, according to the story, could have elapsed since the conquest of Og. How then could his bedstead have been removed in the interval to Rabbath-Ammon, or how could Moses so soon after the event have spoken of

when Rabbah was taken, and this was not till 400 years after the death of Moses, for which see 2 Sam. xii. 26." (P. 41.) Og at all in terms such as these?" (P. 215.)

"You calculate the length of the iron bed of Og the king of Bashan, but you do not prove the bed was too big for the body; you make no allowance for the size of a royal bed, nor even suspect that King Og might have been possessed with the same kind of vanity as Alexander, when he ordered his soldiers to enlarge the size of their beds, that they might give to the Indians in after ages a great idea of the prodigious size of a Macedonian." (Watson, p. 34.) As to its being there unto this day, Moses in his old age made use of a similar expression, when he put the Israelites in mind of what the Lord had done in the Red Sea: "The Lord hath destroyed them *unto this day*." (Deut. xi. 4; Watson, p. 39.) (How is it that both Infidel and Bishop refrain from quoting *this* instance of the phrase?)

"Among the detestable villains that in any period of the world have disgraced the name of man, it is impossible to find a greater than Moses, *if this account be true*.

"Here is an order to *butcher* the boys, to massacre the mothers, and to debauch the daughters. After this order follows an account of the plunder taken, and the manner of dividing it." (P. 40.)

(The remainder of Paine's blackguardism is unquotable;

"How thankful we must be, that we are no longer *obliged to believe as a matter of fact*, of vital consequence to our eternal hope, the story related in Num. xxxi., where we are told that a force of 12,000 Israelites slew *all* the males of the Midianites, and then, by command of Moses, *butchered*, in cold blood, all the women and children, 'except all the women-children who have not known a man by lying with him.' These last the Israelites were to 'keep for

the commencement of this extract is the least objectionable we could find.)

themselves.' . . . . The tragedy of Cawnpore, where 300 were *butchered*, would sink into nothing compared with such a massacre, *if, indeed, we were required to believe it*." (Pp. 143, 144.)

" You think it repugnant to his (God's) moral justice that he should doom to destruction the crying or smiling infants of the Canaanites. Why do you not maintain it to be repugnant to his moral justice that he should suffer crying or smiling infants to be swallowed up by an earthquake, drowned by an inundation, consumed by a fire, starved by a famine, or destroyed by a pestilence? The Canaanites in the time of Moses were idolaters, sacrificers of their own crying or smiling infants, devourers of human flesh; addicted to unnatural lust; immersed in the filthiness of all manner of vice." (Watson, p. 8.) You may as reasonably attribute cruelty and murder to the judge of the land in condemning criminals to death, as butchery and massacre to Moses in executing the command of God (p. 32). The women children were not reserved for purposes of debauchery but of slavery (p. 33).

"The writer has nowhere told us how he came by the speeches which he has put into the mouth of Moses to speak; and therefore we have a right to conclude that he either composed them himself, or wrote them from oral tradition. . . . He has given in the fifth chapter a table of commandments, in which that called the fourth

" That, however, the later Deuteronomist had no very strong sense of the unspeakable sacredness of the earlier document, is sufficiently plain by the liberties he has taken with its contents. . . The latter part of the fourth commandment is completely altered, and a totally different reason is assigned in the passage in Deuteronomy,

commandment is different from the fourth commandment in Exod. xx. *This* makes no mention of the creation; nor *that* of the coming out of Egypt." (P. 37.)

for sanctifying the Sabbath from that laid down in the Book of Exodus, and what is still more remarkable, without any reference to the latter reason as ever existing, Exod. xx. 8—11; Deut. v. 12—15." (P. 361.)

It will be seen by referring to Deut. v. 12, that all that is stated in the passage to have been said by the LORD is "Keep the Sabbath-day to sanctify it." The remainder of the passage is an amplification by Moses, who, knowing that the persons to whom he spoke were already aware of the primary reason for keeping the Sabbath, now urges upon them the fact that they themselves had been *slaves*, as an additional reason for obeying the law, in their treatment of their servants.

"As the writer of the Book of Samuel relates these questions and answers in the language and manner of speaking used in the time they are said to have been spoken, and as that manner of speaking was out of use when this author wrote, he found it necessary, in order to make the story understood, to explain the terms in which the question and answer are spoken, and he does this in the ninth verse, where he says, 'Beforetime in Israel, when a man went to inquire of God,

"Beforetime in Israel when a man went to inquire of God, thus he spake, Come, and let us go to the seer, for he that is now called a prophet (נָבִי Nabi.) was beforetime called a seer" (רֹאֶה, Roeh,) 1 Sam. ix. 9.

"This being the case, it is remarkable that throughout the Pentateuch, and the books of Joshua and Judges the word Roeh is never once used, but Nabi. From this it follows that those portions of these books which contain this later word, as Gen. xx. 7, etc., can hardly

thus he spake, Come, and let us go to the seer: for he that is now called a prophet was beforetime called a seer.' This proves, as I have before said, that this story of Saul, Samuel, and the asses was an ancient story at the time the book of Samuel was written, and consequently that Samuel did not write it." (P. 45.)

have been written before the days of Samuel. In that age the word Nabi may have been known and employed by some, though Roeh was, it seems, the word in popular use. (P. 204.)

" If the blind lead the blind, shall they not both fall into the ditch?" Both writers take the sentence, but to serve different purposes; and both have fallen into the same stupid error. The fact, as we now show, is, that the whole verse in question refers exclusively to Samuel himself, who had been a prophet from his early days; but though a prophet in reality, on account of his youth he had been known by the inferior title of a seer. It must be remembered that Samuel, young as he was, when Eli died, was the only man of God we know of, and we therefore thus read the passage: " Beforetime in Israel when a man went to inquire of God (through young Samuel) thus he spake: Come and let us go to the seer (Samuel), for he (Samuel) that is now called a prophet was beforetime called a seer." During his youth men said of him, Let us go to the *Seer*, but from the time mentioned in 1 Sam. iii. 20, " All Israel knew that Samuel was established to be a *prophet* of the Lord."

" Though it is impossible for us to know *identically* who the writer of Deuteronomy was, it is not difficult to discover here

"From this it follows that those portions of these books which contain this later word, can hardly have been written

professionally that he was some Jewish priest who lived at least 350 years after the time of Moses." (P. 37.) (This is the date of Samuel's life.) before the time of Samuel." (P. 204.)

"The Lord thy God will raise up unto thee a prophet from the midst of thee, of thy brethren, like unto me." "For had ye believed Moses, ye would have believed Me, for *he* wrote of Me." "This is, of a truth, that prophet that should come into the world," Deut. xviii. 15; John v. 46, vi. 14.

But though any Christian would hold that these texts settle the question beyond all dispute, it is not so with Bishop Colenso. We shall, therefore, take one of his own objections next, and in answering it show, as we think certainly, when and where the Pentateuch was written.

"These be the words which Moses spake unto all Israel, *on the other side* בְּעֵבֶר (the English version has, erroneously, 'on this side') *Jordan* in the wilderness," Deut. i. 1.

"*On the other side* Jordan, in the land of Moab, began Moses to declare the law," Deut. i. 5.

It must first be noticed that Bishop Colenso is kind enough to re-translate this passage in i. 1, and print it as, he thinks it ought to be, in i. 5, and in so doing to charge the English Version with error. We shall show that the English translation is right, by very sufficient reasons. Gesenius says the phrase used עֵבֶר הַיַּרְדֵּן "means the region of Palestine beyond Jordan, *i. e.*, situated *to the east of Jordan*." The English version says first on *this* side Jordan, and then more explicitly on *this* side Jordan, *in the plains of Moab*. We also find the same phrase, both in Hebrew and English, used of the place where the tribes of Reuben and Gad asked to have their inheritance fixed, in Num. xxxii. 19, 32, and xxxiv. 15. These *previous* references indisputably prove that the place spoken of was eastward of Jordan, in the after-inheritance of Reuben and Gad. Here, then, the book of Deuteronomy—confessedly the last written of the Pentateuch, even by Dr. Colenso himself—was first spoken, and afterwards written by Moses (Deut. xxxi. 24), and then *delivered publicly to the Levites in the land of Moab.* Consequently it must have been written for, and known to the Israelites, *before they passed over Jordan to possess the promised land.*

This one *fact* completely destroys all Bishop Colenso's *theory*, for it proves by stating the *place where*, the *time when*, and *by whom* this last book of the Pentateuch was written.

We have thus gone through the main points in these two chapters of Bishop Colenso's Second Part, and we see a shameful similarity between the objections of the Infidel of the last, and the Bishop of the present century. We do not assert that Colenso has knowingly borrowed from Paine, both may be indebted to older Infidels; but we will leave the subject to the judgment of the reader, quoting only a few words of Bishop Watson, p. 50, addressed to Paine, which cover the whole ground taken up by Bishop Colenso in these two chapters:—

"A *few verses* in the book of Genesis could not be written by Moses, *therefore no part* of Genesis could be written by Moses. A child would deny your *therefore*."

"CHAPTER VII.

WAS SAMUEL THE ELOHISTIC WRITER OF THE PENTATEUCH?"

IN this chapter of the Bishop's book we arrive at the first portion of positive teaching we have been favoured with. Hitherto the whole of the First and Second Parts have been confined to objections to the truth of the Scripture Narrative; and the setting forth of the theory of Elohistic and Jehovistic writers. Now we have set before us the positive truth to which all the objections hitherto urged have led us, and we must, therefore, consider carefully the extent and value of the theory now fully displayed in this chapter, *i.e.*, that Moses *did not*, because Samuel *did* write the Pentateuch.

And we ask especial notice of the fact, that the whole theory is first propounded in the form of supposition; there is no positive assertion, accompanied by evidence, that the Bishop's statement is correct. In order more fully to display the method used, we shall give the Bishop's theory in his own words, taking the liberty to mark (in italics) the strength of assertion and proof therein displayed. He thus states his case:—" The greater portion of the Pentateuch, at all events, if not, indeed, the *whole* of it (a point which we shall consider more at length hereafter), must have been written at a time later than the age of Moses or Joshua; but, if so, there is no one *mentioned* in the whole history, *before the time of Samuel*, who could be supposed to have written any part of it. We have no sign of any other great prophet in that age, except Deborah, nor of any ' school of the prophets,' existing before his time. That Samuel *did* occupy himself with historical labours we are expressly told in 1 Chron. xxix. 29. In this mention by the Chronicler of the book of Samuel the seer we have, *it may be*, a sign of the activity of Samuel in this direction. This *may also seem to be confirmed* by that other fact recorded about him in 1 Sam. x. 25. And *it is very conceivable* that when he gave up to Saul the reins of government, and during the last thirty-five years of his life, he *may* have devoted himself to such labours as these for the instruction and advancement of his people. In this point of view *there may be* a peculiar significance in the language of the prophet Jeremiah xv. 1, where he closely couples Samuel with *Moses*—' Then said Jehovah unto me, Though Moses and Samuel stood before Me, yet my mind could not be toward this people."

" In such a work as this Samuel *may have been* aided by the sons of the prophets, who *clearly must have had* some sort of occupation besides that of merely prophesying, *i.e.*, *probably* chanting psalms and joining in religious processions.

"*It is very possible* that Samuel *may have* gathered in those schools some of the more promising young men of his time, and *may have* endeavoured to train them, to the best of his power, in such knowledge of every kind as he himself had acquired—the art of *writing it may be*, among the rest. In short, these schools *may have* resembled a modern college. For their use, in the first instance, he *may have* composed, from whatever resources he had at command, either from the traditions of the people, or *it may be, as far as we know at present*, with the help of written documents handed down from an earlier time, some account of the earlier history of Israel. *It is possible*, in fact, that at the time when his sons, set up by himself as judges in Beersheba, turned aside after lucre, and took bribes, and perverted judgment (1 Sam. viii. 3), Samuel *may have been* too closely engaged, and his attention too much absorbed, in such matters as these, to correct such disorders. Among his pupils, *probably*, as we have just said, were Nathan and Gad themselves, who thus *may have had* their first lessons in the writing of history.

"Hitherto we have been advancing upon *certain* ground." " But we are now entering on the field of conjecture." " For myself, at all events, it would be a sinful shutting of my eyes to the plain light of Truth, if I ventured any longer to maintain the usual opinions as to the origin and composition of the Pentateuch."

The reader is referred to Chapter XX. to see into what a ridiculous snare Dr. Colenso deliberately asserts he has walked with his eyes open. But, meanwhile, here, "provisionally and tentatively," as the Bishop words it, borrowing from Holyoake's description of Secularism, we have the Primary Instalment of the New Religion. We know exactly what we are called upon to give up, and to receive instead, in this first stage of New Development.

The assertion is, that Samuel wrote the Pentateuch, in part at least; and the proof of the assertion, as Bishop Colenso has offered it, we have given above. Throughout, there is nothing but the mere suggestion of probability; every sentence, every suggestion, is guarded with a *may be;* every door is left open for a retreat when necessary. The fact of who is *not* the writer of the Pentateuch has been very loudly proclaimed; but who *did* write it is, at first, suggested in the merest and most uncertain whisperings of probability, the most timid suggestions of what may have been.

There is not one fact of history, not one legend, not one tradition brought forward in support of Bishop Colenso's view. He has said Samuel wrote the Pentateuch, and the proof he offers is *these suggestions of his own;*—that Moses did not write it; that it must have been written about the time of Samuel; that there was no one else living about that time, *that we know of,* who could have written it; therefore, it must have been written by Samuel!

There is, then, not a scintilla of evidence offered by Bishop Colenso in support of his theory that Samuel wrote the Pentateuch. It must be received on the bare assertion of the Bishop, or not received at all.

We shall now proceed to give a rapid summary of the evidence that Moses wrote the Pentateuch, and, in so doing, shall have to show what Dr. Colenso rejects as a "sinful shutting of his eyes to the truth." For convenience of illustration, we shall divide our summary into three parts ("a threefold cord is not easily broken"):—I. The Heathen; II. The Jewish; III. The Christian Testimonies in favour of Moses as the writer of the Pentateuch.

I. The Heathen testimony that Moses was the writer of the Pentateuch.—Juvenal, Justin the abbreviator of Trogus, Strabo, Diodorus Siculus, Tacitus, Artapanus, Eupolemus, Manetho, beside many other writers of antiquity, all testify that Moses was the leader of the Jews and the founder of their laws. The Egyptians, as Josephus asserts, esteemed him to be a wonderful and divine man, and were willing to have him thought a priest of their own, which certainly was a proof of their high opinion of him, though mixed with other fabulous relations. The great critic Longinus, extolling those who represent the Deity as he really is— pure, great, and unmixed—testifies that thus did the legislator of the Jews, who, he says, was no ordinary man, but as he conceived so he spoke worthily of the power of God. The same writer expressly commends the words in Gen. i., "Let there be light." Numenius, the Pythagorean philosopher, of Apamea, in Syria, called Moses a man most powerful in prayer to God, and said, "What is Plato but Moses speaking in the Attic dialect?" this sentiment, whether just or not, is a proof of this philosopher's high opinion of Moses.

Further, Porphyry, one of the most acute and learned enemies of Christianity, admitted the genuineness of the Pentateuch, and acknowledged that Moses was prior to the Phœnician historian Sanconiathon, who lived before the Trojan War. He even contended for the truth of Sanconiathon's account of the Jews, *from its coincidence with the Mosaic history*. Nor was the genuineness of the Pentateuch denied by any of the numerous writers against the Gospel during the first four centuries of the Christian era, although the fathers constantly appealed to the histories and prophecies of the Old Testament in support of the divine origin of the doctrines which they taught. The power of historical truth compelled the Emperor Julian, whose favour to the Jews appears to have proceeded solely from his hostility to the Christians, to acknowledge that persons instructed by the Spirit of God once lived among the Israelites; and to confess that the books which bore the name of Moses were genuine, and that the facts they contained were worthy of credit. Mahomet maintained the inspiration of Moses, and revered the sanctity of the Jewish laws. Manetho, Berosus, and many others, give accounts confirming, and according with, the Mosaic history.

II. The Jewish testimony that Moses was the writer of the Pentateuch.—"Is there any value in their testimony?" may be inquired. "Are they not certain to bear witness to anything that may appear to enhance the antiquity of their race, and their consequent importance in the history of the world?" The answer is simple and convincing. The Jews, in preserving the Pentateuch, have, through all the dull gray mists of the hoary centuries during which it has existed, preserved a stern and unswerving witness against themselves and their idolatries in the first instance, and their rejection of the true Messiah in the last. Thoroughly to appreciate the value of the evidence we now submit, it must be remembered how hard the Mosaic law bore upon the personal freedom of the Jew. Three times in the year, at whatever inconvenience, they were to appear in a certain place; every seventh year they were to keep as a Sabbath; they must not employ cavalry in their wars. And as the whole Jewish people were made the depositories and keepers of their laws, it is therefore impossible to conceive that any nation, with such motives to reject, and such opportunities of detecting forged documents, should receive them, and submit to the heavy yoke contained in them.

The first evidence we take from the Jewish Confession of Faith, commonly used in the present day, which carries us back at one step to the thirteenth century. We quote the 7th and 8th articles only :—

"I firmly believe, that all the prophecies of Moses our Master

(God rest his soul in peace!) are true, and that he is the father of all the sages, whether they went before or follow after him.

"*I firmly believe, that the Law* [Pentateuch] *which we have now in our hands was given by Moses;* God rest his soul in peace!"

The next backward step, to the first century of the Christian era, is attested by two witnesses. Philo, an Egyptian Jew, who then lived, quoted, as having canonical authority, no other books than those which are contained in the Hebrew Bible. And we have also the writings of Josephus, himself a Jewish priest, contemporary with the apostles. To understand his testimony, the reader must be acquainted with the fact, that the thirty-nine books of the English Bible are all (neither more nor less) compressed into twenty-two books of the Hebrew Scriptures. Josephus says, in his treatise against Apion, "We have not thousands of books, discordant, and contradicting each other; but we have only *twenty-two*, which comprehend the history of all ages, and are justly regarded as divine. *Five of them proceed from Moses;* they include as well the *Laws*, as an account of the creation of man, extending to the time of his death."

Before passing the Christian era, it is necessary to mention the Talmud and the Mishna. From the second century and onward an increasing number of Jewish writers busied themselves with oral explanations of the Torah, or law of Moses, and the systematic collection of them afterwards called Mishna. Fearing that the oral law which they held so sacred should be lost or impaired, the Jews during the second century thought of committing it to writing. Rabbi Judah, surnamed the Holy, made the permanent record of it. It will be seen from an extract from the Mishna at the end of this section, that it is clearly stated therein that Moses wrote the law. A twofold commentary, or series of commentaries, was subsequently appended to it; one called the Babylonian *Gemara*, the other the Jerusalem *Gemara*.

The former was begun by Rabbi Asche, and was completed by Rabbi Jose, who died A.D. 475. The portions, committed to writing after the Mishna, constitute *notes* on that text, and make up together with it the Babylonian Talmud. The *Gemara* of the Jerusalem Talmud proceeded from the academy at Tiberias, and embodied the notes of the Palestinian Jews. It is attributed to Rabbi Jochanan, who died in A.D. 279. This *Gemara* with the same Mishna as before makes up *the Jerusalem Talmud.*

The next step brings us to the time and into the very presence of our Lord. The Sadducees of his time received as canonical the *five books of Moses only*; they appealed to them in every dispute, they bowed only to decisions that could be thereby established, they were their peculiar study, the source of their doctrines, and the only authoritative guide they acknowledged. Yet amongst this sect the question was never mooted as to the authorship of the Pentateuch; one and all, without exception, ascribed it to Moses.

About fifty years before the time of Christ were written the Targums of Onkelos on the Pentateuch, and of Jonathan ben Uzziel on the Prophets; in both these works the Pentateuch is said to be written by Moses.

The Book of Ecclesiasticus was written in the Syro-Chaldaic dialect, about 232 years before Christ, and was translated by the grandson of Jesus, the author, into Greek, for the use of the Alexandrian Jews. The translator says, that (Torah) *the Law* and the Prophets were studied by his grandfather, and they were therefore certainly extant at that time.

Fifty years before the age of the author of Ecclesiasticus, about B.C. 282, the Greek version of the Old Testament (commonly known as the Septuagint) was executed at Alexandria, the books of which are the same as in our Bible, and consequently in their text they join with our Version and the Hebrew in testifying that Moses wrote the Pentateuch. From this point it is impossible to ascend higher, except by appeal to the Old Testament and Jewish tradition, as no authentic books whatever are extant.

The completion of the Canon of the Old Testament denotes the next step in historic retrogression, and we ask especial notice of the completeness, step by step, of the Jewish testimony in favour of the Mosaic authorship of the Pentateuch.

The Canon of the Old Testament was completed by Ezra, who, with the assistance of the members of the Great Synagogue, (among whom were the prophets Haggai, Zechariah, and Malachi) collected as many copies of the sacred writings as he could, and from them set forth a correct edition of the canon of the Old Testament; with the exception of his own writings, the book of Nehemiah, and the prophecy of Malachi; which were subsequently annexed to the canon by Simon the Just, who is said to have been the last of the Great Synagogue. In the Esdrine text the errors of the former copyists were corrected, and Ezra (being himself an inspired writer) added in several places throughout the books of this edition what was necessary to illustrate, connect, or complete them. Whether Ezra's own copy of the Jewish Scriptures perished in the pillage of the temple by Antiochus Epiphanes is a question that cannot now be ascertained, nor is it material, since we know that Judas Maccabeus repaired the temple, and replaced everything requisite for the performance of divine worship, which included a correct, if not Ezra's own, copy of the Scriptures. It is not improbable that in this latter temple an ark was constructed, in which the sacred books of the Jews were preserved until the destruction of Jerusalem, and the subversion of the Jewish polity by the Romans under Titus, before whom *the volume of the law was carried in triumph* among the other spoils which had been taken at Jerusalem.

The remainder of the Jewish testimony must now be gathered from the text itself.

Ezra, who has often been set forward as the writer of the Pentateuch, expressly ascribes the book of the law to Moses, vi. 18; he lived B.C. 537 or 538. Long before that event it was extant in the time of Josiah, B.C. 624, and was then of such acknowledged authority that the perusal of it occasioned an immediate reformation in the religious usages. It was extant in the time of Hoshea, King of Israel, B.C. 678, since a captive priest was sent back from Babylon to instruct the new colonists of Samaria in the religion which it teaches. By these Samaritans it was preserved and handed down to their posterity, as it also was by the Jews, as the basis of the civil and religious institutions of both nations. It was extant in the time of Jehoshaphat, King of Judah, B.C. 912, who employed public instructors for its promulgation. And since the Pentateuch was received as the law by the ten tribes, and also by the two tribes, it follows as a necessary consequence that they each received it *before* they became divided into two kingdoms; for if it had been forged in a later age among the Jews, the perpetual enmity that subsisted between them and the Israelites would have utterly prevented it from being adopted by the Samaritans, and had it been a spurious production of the Samaritans it would never have been received by the Jews. *There remains, therefore, only one resource to those who contend that Moses was not the author; namely, that it was written in the period which elapsed between the age of Joshua and that of Solomon.*

But the whole Jewish history, from the time of this settlement in Canaan to the building of the temple at Jerusalem, pre-supposes that the book of the law was written by Moses. The whole of the temple service and worship was regulated by Solomon, B.C. 1004, according to the law contained in the Pentateuch, as the Tabernacle service and worship had previously been by David, B.C. 1042. Could Solomon indeed have persuaded his subjects that for more than five hundred years the worship and polity prescribed in the Pentateuch had been religiously observed by their ancestors, if it had not been observed? Could he have imposed upon them concerning the antiquity of the Sabbath, of circumcision, and of their three great festivals? In fact, it is morally impossible that any forgery could have been executed by or in the time of Solomon. Moreover, that the Pentateuch was extant in the time of David is evident from the very numerous allusions made in his psalms to its contents. But it could not have been drawn up by him, since the law contained in the Pentateuch, forbids many practices of which David was guilty.

SAMUEL (who judged Israel about the years, B.C. 1100—1060) *could not have acquired the knowledge of Egypt which the Pentateuch implies;* for Herodotus tells us that Egyptian learning was carefully concealed from foreigners. The priests alone, and the royal family, who were reckoned as priests, had access to it. *To this class, therefore, the writer must have belonged,* and every child knows that Moses was for many years the adopted son of Pharaoh's daughter.

In the Book of Joshua (which, though reduced to its present form in later times, was undoubtedly composed in respect to its essential parts at a very early period) frequent references may be found to the book of the law in Josh. i. 7, 8, xxiii. 6, xxiv. 6. The Pentateuch, therefore, was extant in the time of Joshua.

To Moses alone, indeed, can the Pentateuch be attributed, and this indirect evidence from tradition is stronger than a more direct and positive ascription, which would have been the obvious resource of fraud.

We will conclude this second branch of the testimony by placing before the readers a copy of the Jewish record of the actual persons to whom the copies of the Book of the Law (Torah—Pentateuch) have been officially entrusted from the time of Moses himself to the close of the canon by the members of the Great Synagogue, of whom the last was Simon the Just, and from thence onward to the completion of the Talmud.

This extract was copied by one of the authors of this work from the Mishna in a Jewish synagogue in London, on Sunday, February 8, 1863, and an English translation is appended made by the same workman who took the copy.

משה קבל תורה מסני ׳ ומסרה ליהושע ׳ ויהושע ליזקנאים ׳
וזקנאים לנביאים ׳ ונבאים לאנשי כנסת הגדולה ׳שמעון הצדק
היה משירי כנסת הגדולה ׳ אנטיגנוס איש סוכו קבל מהם ׳
ויכו בן יוחנן קבל מהם ׳ ויהשוע בן פרחיה קבל מהם ׳
ויהודה בן טבאי קבל מהם ׳ שמעיה קבל מהם ׳ הלל קבל
מהם ׳ רב גמליאל קבל מהם ׳ שמעון בנו קבל מהם ׳ רבי
קבל מהם ׳ יהודה בן המא קבל מהם :
רב אשי מתלמיד קבל מהם :
מישניות : סדר נזיקון פרק אבות.

Moses received the law from Sinai, he gave it to Joshua, who gave it to the elders, the elders to the prophets, the prophets to the great men of the congregation, of whom Simon the Just was the last remaining. Simon the Just gave it to Antigonus, the man of Soko; Josa, the son of Jochanan, received it from Antigonus; Joshua, the son of Parachiah, received it from Josu; Judah, the son of Taba, received it from Joshua; Shemaiah received it from Judah; Hillel received it from Shemaiah; Rab. Gamaliel received it from Hillel; Simon, the son of Gamaliel, received it from Gamaliel; Rabbi received it from Simon; Judah the son of Thama, received it from Rabbi; (Judah was the last of the men who wrote the Mishna), and Rabbi Asche was the compiler of the Talmud.—Taken from "Mishna; Pirke Aboth."

It must be noticed that in the above the names from Antigonus downward are in the plural, because each man mentioned was at the head of a school.

Before leaving this unbroken chain of evidence, it may be well to point out the exceedingly small number of persons through whom tradition would have to be passed from Adam to Moses, as follows—Adam, Methuselah, Shem, Isaac, Levi, Amram, Moses. Through the agency of six men, therefore, Moses might, and most probably did, receive all the accounts needed by him for the preparation of the history of the world from the creation to his own days.

III. It would be utterly impossible for us to mention the Christian writers who during eighteen centuries have expressed their belief that the Pentateuch was written by Moses; we shall, therefore, simply summarize the New Testament testimony to the Mosaic authorship of the Pentateuch. There are in the different books of the New Testament ninety quotations from the Pentateuch. Every one of the writers, without exception, makes one or more quotations from it, appealing to it as law, unquestionable and divine. John the beloved disciple, and Paul, who last saw Jesus, declare positively that Moses was the writer of the Pentateuch; and, best of all, our Lord Himself, whose lightest word should settle such a question for ever, declares in fourteen different instances that Moses wrote the Pentateuch.

Thus the Heathen and the Jew, the Christian, the Apostles, and the Lord of Glory,—the power *and wisdom of God—all* bear unvarying and harmonious testimony to the fact that Moses wrote the books of the Pentateuch.

That Samuel wrote them we have the unsupported assertion of the Bishop of Natal, who has in Chap. XX. *demonstrated the absolute impossibility of the truth of his own assertion.*

"CHAPTER VIII.

INTRODUCTION OF THE NAME JEHOVAH."

THE Bishop thus states this subject—" In the story of the Exodus we read as follows : 'And God spake unto Moses, and said unto him, I am JEHOVAH. And I appeared unto Abraham, unto Isaac, and unto Jacob, by the name of God Almighty (EL SHADDAI), but by my name Jehovah was I not known to them. And I have also established my covenant with them, to give them the land of Canaan, the land of their pilgrimage, wherein they were strangers,' etc., Ex. vi. 2—8. The above passage cannot, as it seems to me, without a perversion of its obvious meaning—the meaning which would be ascribed to it by the great body of simple-minded readers, who have never had their attention awakened to the difficulties in which the whole narrative becomes involved thereby—be explained to say anything else than this, that the name Jehovah was not known at all to the patriarchs, but was now for the first time revealed as the name by which the God of Israel would be henceforth distinguished from all other gods."

" So Professor Lee admits, who in his Hebrew Lexicon explains the word Jehovah to " be the most sacred and inalienable name of God, unknown, however, to the patriarchs; *it is not therefore more ancient in all probability than the time of Moses.*" And so Josephus writes, *Ant.* ii. 12—4,—" Wherefore God declared to him (Moses) his holy name, which had never been discovered to men before." But then we come at once upon the contradictory fact, that the name Jehovah is repeatedly used in the earlier parts of the story, throughout the whole book of Genesis. And it is not merely employed by the writer, when relating simply, as an historian, in his own person, events of a more ancient date, in which case he might be supposed to have introduced the word, as having become, in his own day, after having been thus revealed, familiar to himself and his readers; but it is put into the mouths of the patriarchs themselves, as Abraham, Gen. xiv. 22; Isaac, xxvi. 22; Jacob, xxviii. 16. Nay, according to the story, it was not only known to these, but to a multitude of others. So, too, in all the Elohistic portions of the book of Genesis, in some of which a multitude of names occur, and many of them compounded with the Divine name EL, there is not a single one compounded with the name JEHOVAH, in the form either of the prefix *Jeho* or *Jo*, or the termination *Jah*, both of which are so commonly employed in later times. Thus there are thirteen names in Gen. v., sixteen in Gen. xi., fifteen in Gen. xxii., thirty-three in Gen. xxv., seventy in Gen. xlvi., in all one hundred and forty-seven names, and in the last of these passages we have Israel, Jemuel, Jahliel, Machiel, Jahzeel; but *in not a single instance is any of these names compounded with the word Jehovah.*" The Bishop evidently thinks he has a strong point in this assertion, for he repeats it many times under different forms, as for instance:—" If so many names were formed, before the times of Moses compounded with *El*, how is it that not one, throughout the whole book of Genesis, is compounded with Jehovah, on the supposition that this name was known and used so freely from the first?"

We have therefore to take into consideration, first, the introduction of the name Jehovah, and next the Bishop's clear *assertion*, that in not a single instance in Genesis is any of these names compounded with the word Jehovah. The formidable difficulty, as the Bishop puts it, must be first considered, and as it is specially commended to " simple-minded readers," we are the very persons, of all others, to say a few words upon it.

Here is the difficulty in few words. God speaking of Abraham,

Isaac, and Jacob, says, "By my name Jehovah was I not known to them," while, in fact, to almost every person in Genesis the name seems commonly known. We do not think this objection is to be found in Paine's work, but we have heard it propounded as a knotty point at Infidel Lectures, years ago, and we shall therefore repeat here the explanation we have, in part, given there.

There are two ways of dissolving it; the first is to suppose that Moses was speaking proleptically throughout the narrative in Genesis; but as this explanation found no favour in our simple minds, we have abandoned it for one more simple and satisfactory.

Let us now see the exact words used; and be it observed that no Hebrew is needed here, nor is any violence to the text required:—" And God spake unto Moses, and said unto him, I am the LORD. And I appeared unto Abraham, unto Isaac, and unto Jacob by God Almighty, but by my name JEHOVAH was I not known to them."

First we observe that in this verse there are two very distinct things mentioned—the *appearance* of God under one name, and the *knowledge* of Him under another. There is the appearance of El Shaddai, the Almighty Creator, who at various times and in divers manners was pleased personally to manifest Himself to those whom He had formed in his own image, and there is the knowledge of Him in his more abstract being as the Uncreated Lord God, from Everlasting to Everlasting, as the Hebrew original of the words translated " I Am that I Am," so grandly but simply expresses.

Noting these differences brings us to the second thought, that instead of the verse being one continued declaration throughout, as the Bishop has put it, it really consists of two parts— a declaration followed by a question. The declaration is first made, " I *appeared* unto Abraham, unto Isaac, and unto Jacob, by God Almighty ;" and then the question follows: " But by my name Jehovah was I not *known* to them ?" Simply to place the words thus in an interrogative form, dissolves entirely the Bishop's difficulty, and destroys the theory founded thereupon. And that the word "not," here used, will bear the interpretation we have thus given, can be proved by multitudes of instances in God's Holy Word, of which we now quote a few examples: " If thou doest well shalt thou not be accepted?" Gen. iv. 7; "Said he not unto me, she is my sister?" Gen. xx. 5; "Told not I thee saying all that the Lord speaketh?" Num. xxiii. 26; "Have not I commanded thee?" Josh. i. 9; "Is it not written in the book of Joshua?" Josh. x. 14; "Hearest thou not, my daughter?" Ruth ii. 8; "Hast thou not there with thee Zadok and Abiathar?" 2 Sam. xv. 35; "Are they not written in the book?" 2 Kings xx. 20; "Dost thou not watch over my sin?" Job xiv. 16; "Is not God in the height of heaven?" Job xxii. 12; "Doth not wisdom cry?" Prov. viii. 1; " Do they not err that devise evil?" Prov. xiv. 22; "Have not I written?" Prov. xxii. 20. In all these instances the word "not" is used in precisely the same manner as in the words we are considering, " By my name Jehovah was I not known to them ?"

The construction of the whole verse shows that these words do not form the completion of the previous declaration; but that the question is simply and naturally led up to by the consideration of the facts previously recorded.

It is also to be remarked, carefully, that the Bishop has not quoted any one text to show that the view he has taken is correct. It is an old and valuable canon of Scripture criticism, that no great principle or doctrine is left upon a single Scripture; that whenever anything of importance is mentioned, it is always reiterated in some form or other. This being the well-known fact, we are entitled to ask for the corroborating Scripture that confirms the Bishop's view. We are bold to assert that it cannot be found. We have quoted thirteen Scriptures to support our view of the subject, and might easily have trebled the number.

Thus viewed, this *question* forms a part of a great and harmonious whole—the peculiar name of the Lord God Almighty, that by which He had been known to Abraham, Isaac, and Jacob, is to form the credentials of the former Egyptian prince to his oppressed and suffering countrymen. Especially known to their fathers by that name, which was and is, His alone, Jehovah Elohim would come to their rescue, and for their release do battle with the false gods of Egypt.

Having thus shown that there is nothing in this text to militate against the statement of the early knowledge of the name Jehovah, and by so doing dissolved the Bishop's objection, we now pass to consider his assertion: "There are seventy names in Gen. xlvi." "but *in not a single instance is any of these names compounded with the word Jehovah.*"

To show the untruthfulness of this audacious assertion, we must return to the Hebrew text; and it is to be noticed that the Bishop's objection is gone, and his assertion proved untrue, if only one instance is produced, one single name in Gen. xlvi. proved to be compounded with Jehovah. It must first be remarked that the Bishop has taken for granted that the syllables which in our English version form the name Jehovah, are identical with those of the Hebrew text. This is as far as possible from being the case. To form syllables vowels are necessary. The vowels that form the name Jehovah in the Hebrew are unknown. The vowels to the words Elohim, or Adonai, are commonly used where necessary; but every Jewish child is aware that there are no vowels known, as belonging to the peculiar name—Jehovah.

It will thus be seen in the outset that any statement founded upon such unknown vowels, must be received with the greatest caution. But the consonants of the name are fixed, known, and unalterable; and it is to these we must look for the identification of any name with that of Jehovah. In one minute their form may be learned, as here subjoined (יהוה); and we ask our reader to learn them before proceeding further—remembering that they read from right to left.

The Bishop states, and repeats, and founds his objection upon this—that we cannot find *any* name in Gen. xlvi. *that is compounded with these letters.* In reply, short and simple, we point out one name *that contains them all,* Judah (יהודה), where any one may see and understand, that by taking away the fourth of these letters (reading in the Hebrew manner, from right to left) the whole name of Jehovah (יהוה) stands revealed; and that every letter is in its proper place, without even a transposition. By looking to the margin of the English version (Gen. xxix. 35) it will be seen that this word Judah is translated "praise;" but the full meaning of the name is *as Leah gives it in the same verse*—Jehovah praised. With this one fact known, we may well wonder at the audacity of the assertion the Bishop has ventured upon, and reiterated again and again; and we may ask what is the critical value of the book that contains such an assertion.

But this is not the only instance. There is also the name Joseph, which is thus written, in Hebrew, in Gen. xlvi., the chapter in question (יוסף), and is composed of the same number of letters as יהוה. It will be seen that the first and second of Joseph are the first and third of Jehovah. The full meaning and translation of this name Joseph is quoted in the words of his mother, Rachel, at the time of his birth—*i. e.,* "Jehovah shall add," translated in the English Bible, Gen. xxx. 24, margin, "adding."

We come now to the *third* instance, where the Bishop asserts *there are none.* In Gen. xlvi. 13, the name of Job is mentioned, written thus (יוב). This case is exactly parallel with that of Joseph, in connection with the name יהוה. Job consisting of three letters, of which the first and second are the same as the first and third of the Divine name.

The *fourth* instance is in the name in the tenth verse, Jemuel, ימואל, which contains the first and third letters as before.

There are also fifth and sixth instances of the compounding in the same verse in the names Jamin (ימין), and Jachin (יכין), both of which contain the whole of the Divine name written with the double י (thus יי), which is the common way of contracting the name in use amongst the Jews, and which any Jew would instantly recognize.

We suppose that *these six instances thus quoted from the chapter where the Bishop asserts there is not one*, will be sufficient to prove the absolute untruthfulness of his assertion, and consequently to overthrow the theory he has founded upon it.

It is, also, easy to discover the snare into which he has fallen headlong, and to point it out, by stating, that in the Lexicon of Gesenius the translations in full, as above given, are not inserted; consequently any person ignorant of the minutiæ of the Hebrew language, and trusting to Gesenius, must fall into exactly the same pit as Dr. Colenso has fallen into.

It must also be further noticed that the Bishop's theory is *founded upon syllables which are not in existence*, since no living man can prove *any syllable whatever* as forming part of the Divine name known amongst us as Jehovah.

Thus, at one sweep, the whole argument founded upon the late adoption of the syllables of the name Jehovah is set aside by stating the fact that such syllables are not now, and never were, known to be in existence.

Indeed, before Bishop Colenso, or any one else, is in a position to prove any argument founded upon the syllables of this divine name, he must be able to say what the syllables are, which we take to be an insuperable difficulty. The English Version has Jehovah; the Hebrew Bible has the name confessedly compounded with the vowels of other words—Elohim or Adonai. All the Hebrew commentators agree that there are no vowels known to be connected with the name of Jehovah; and we end our chapter by asking Dr. Colenso, before adopting any argument founded upon the syllables of the divine name, to tell us whether there are two, or three, or four syllables in the name יהוה.

"CHAPTER IX.

THE DERIVATION OF THE NAME MORIAH."

This chapter is a continuation of the previous subject.—The introduction of the name Jehovah, and finding the syllables composing that name in the names of places and persons of that time.

· We shall therefore place one statement from the previous chapter in company with the instance—the name Moriah—to which the Bishop has devoted the whole of this chapter of his work.

In the course of our remarks upon these subjects, we hope to prove that the foundation upon which the Bishop builds is not trustworthy, that his statements are unreliable, and that he has fallen into a snare through deficient acquaintance with the minutiæ of the Hebrew language: we therefore quote as follows from Chapter VIII.:—"There are only two names of persons throughout the whole Pentateuch and Book of Joshua which are compounded with Jehovah—viz., that of *Jo*shua himself, and

E

probably that of Jochebed the mother of Moses;" and continuing this theme in Chapter IX., the Bishop proceeds: "There is however one word in Genesis, the name of a place, מוֹרִיָּה, Moriah, Gen. xxii. 2, which appears at first sight to be compounded with Jehovah. HENGSTENBERG, i., 274—277, insists very strongly on this point, and for the sake of the Hebrew student and critic, we must consider his arguments at length. For the ordinary reader, however, it will be sufficient to observe as follows:—

"(I.) *This is the* ONLY *instance in the whole book of Genesis where any name of place or person is* (*apparently*) *compounded with the name Jehovah.*

"(II.) It is *most unlikely* that this place was generally known (as the Divine command in verse 2—' Get thee into the land of Moriah'—evidently implies), known, therefore, to the idolatrous Canaanites, by a name compounded with Jehovah, when there is not a single other instance, in the whole Bible, of the existence of another name so compounded in that age.

"(III.) It is impossible that the place could have been already known familiarly as 'Moriah,' which means, according to HENGSTENBERG, 'appearance of Jehovah,' *before* that very 'appearance of Jehovah' took place, described in the story, Gen. xxii., to which the giving of the name itself is ascribed.

"(IV.) It is shown below, on critical grounds, that the word in question, מוֹרִיָּה, cannot be formed as HENGSTENBERG supposes."

In entering upon the consideration of these various topics, we call attention to the utter lack of truth in the assertion, " There are only *two* names of persons compounded with Jehovah throughout the whole Pentateuch and Book of Joshua—viz., Joshua and Jochebed."

In the previous chapter we have shown *six instances* of compounding with Jehovah in Genesis, where the Bishop says there are none—*i. e.*, Judah, Joseph, Job, Jemuel, Jamin, and Jachin. But these last two are founded upon an usage of the Hebrew, of which the Bishop is evidently ignorant, and which we may therefore consider (in fairness to him) is not to be found amongst his German-Hebrew fellow critics. It will consequently be necessary for us, if we would be believed, to explain and to prove the position we have taken, in asserting them to contain the name Jehovah.

We assert, then, that the *syllables* Jo, Jeho, Jah, though commonly used, have no known authorized foundation, as forming part of the word Jehovah, and this we show beyond dispute, by stating the fact, that no living man will undertake to prove, how many syllables are contained in the divine name of the four letters (יהוה).

If this statement is true, and *every lexicon* we can find, *every authority*, Jewish and Christian, we can trace, bear concurrent witness to its truth, then any system founded upon the syllables must, necessarily, fall to the ground, as having no foundation to rest upon.

But this statement concerns the syllables only; and though it disposes at once of the case submitted in this chapter, does not touch the name as a whole. We now come, therefore, to the name as a whole, and shall add one or two more instances to the six already produced, to further establish the want of truth in the Bishop's assertion, and to prove authoritatively the position we are now taking.

We have said in the previous chapter that by the usage of the Hebrew language, the letter י twice written or printed is a contraction of the name Jehovah; thus יי is יהוה contracted; and we have given *two* instances where it is so used. We now give a *third* instance from the Book of Genesis, and prove the whole usage by a fourth instance taken from the Book of Numbers.

The name now given is utterly subversive of the whole theory of the late date of the formation of the name Jehovah, inasmuch as in the present instance it is in the name of Cain's great grandson, מְחִיָּיאֵל (Mehujael), who lived long before the Flood, that the contracted name of יהיה is found. In this very ancient name it will be seen that the two central י's form the name Jehovah, and therefore the whole of this magnificent name signifies, "proclaiming Jehovah God."

The fourth instance of this contraction is found in the name of Jair, the son of Manasseh, mentioned in Numb. xxxii. 41, and thus spelt in Hebrew (יָאִיר), and by quoting this instance we shall be able to show authority in support of this usage of double י that the Bishop will not, we think, venture to dispute.

In the translation of this name in Gesenius's Hebrew and Chaldee Lexicon, p. 326, it is thus explained: יָאִיר, "whom He (*i. e.*, God) enlightens;" and it must be remarked that in this name, there is no other trace of the divine name than the use of the י here doubled; but many writers say that a single י at the commencement of a proper name is a contraction of Jehovah. (See Jones's "Hebrew Names," art. Jehovah.)

In Bagster's Hebrew-English Lexicon, p. 102, it is thus given, יָאִיר (the Lord enlightens, Ιάειρος).

In the Jewish Commentaries יי is commonly used in the notes as a contraction of יהוה, see (for instance) De Sola on Genesis, xxii. 14, note, where יי יראה is used for יהוה יראה (Jehovah Jireh).

We have thus particularized eight distinct instances of the compounding of the name Jehovah, where the Bishop asserts and reiterates again and again that there are none; and those instances extend upward from the time of Moses to the date of Adam's existence upon the earth; further, the name of Mehujael and the compounding of Jehovah therein manifest, proves that this divine name was known to, and used by the Patriarchs *before the Flood.*

Having thus conclusively shown the untruthfulness of the Bishop's assertion, we now proceed to the main subject of this chapter: the derivation of the name Moriah—of which the Bishop remarks:—

(I.) " This is the *only* instance in the whole Book of Genesis where any name of place or person is apparently compounded with Jehovah."

We reply that we have shown *seven other instances*, as above, consequently that the assertion is an untruth, originating, as we believe, in ignorance.

(II.) " It is *most unlikely* that this place was generally known unto the idolatrous Canaanites by a name compounded with Jehovah, when there is not a single other instance in the whole Bible, of the existence of another name so compounded in that age."

It does not follow because Abraham knew the place called the land of Moriah by that name, that therefore it was known as such by the idolatrous Canaanites; neither is it asserted in the Narrative that they did know anything about it. The name by which the land of Moriah appears to have been known among the Canaanites was " Jebus, which is Jerusalem."—See Jud. xix. 10.

The command is from God to Abraham, and no one else is apparently concerned in the matter. This is a sample of the Bishop's mode of proceeding; where he wishes to have a difficulty, and cannot find it, he *makes* it for the occasion.

(III.) " It is impossible that the place could have been already familiarly known as Moriah, which means, according to Hengstenberg, ' appearance of Jehovah,' before that very appearance of Jehovah took place described in the story, Gen. xxii., to which the giving of the name itself is ascribed."

This brings us to the real purpose of this chapter, which consists of two parts: the first, that the name Moriah cannot have been known at the time it was spoken; the second, that the name Moriah could not be formed so as to be compounded with Jehovah.

The real questions at issue are: Was this place called Moriah at all at this time? and, Can the name Moriah be shown to be compounded with Jehovah? It is distinctly stated in Gen. xxii., that the Lord said unto Abraham, Get thee into the land of Moriah; then, that Abraham journeyed for two days, and on the third saw the place that had been already named, and which was known to him, or was then made known to him, as the place indicated; so that it would appear impossible that the place was called Moriah in consequence of this transaction. Nor does the Narrative, either here or elsewhere, state that it was so. Was there, then, any former transaction which could have obtained this name for the land in question? The Narrative upon this point is silent; but Jewish tradition states, "Moriah was also the place on which Adam, Hebel (Abel), and Noach (Noah) offered sacrifices." This tradition sufficiently accounts for the name of Moriah being well known to Abraham, previous to the issuing of the commandment to offer up Isaac there. We are, consequently, quite at liberty to believe that the name Moriah may have been commonly known as the designation of the mountain region, upon one of the peaks of which the Temple of Solomon was afterwards built. Indeed, the only reason why we should not fully believe it, is, the Bishop's theory will not allow of it; but we think we have utterly destroyed that theory on very different grounds.

The second question is, Can the name Moriah be shown to be compounded with the syllables of Jehovah?

Our answer to this is, The syllables have no authority whatever, and consequently no argument worth holding can be carried on concerning them; we will therefore simply point out that the Hebrew word used is not Moriah merely, as in the English Version, but Mori-yah, or Mori-jah, having certainly in its final syllable the first two letters of יהוה, namely יה. We refrain from pursuing this part of the inquiry, because Bishop Colenso says, "We do not profess to be able to give with certainty the true origin and meaning of the word," to which, notwithstanding this admission, a chapter of eight pages is entirely devoted.

Not only so, but the Bishop admits that "ver. 14 does not expressly state that the name 'Moriah' was formed on this occasion. It says, Abraham called the name of that place, not Moriah, but Jehovah Jireh, with express reference to the proverb, As it is said, In the Mount of Jehovah it (*or He*) shall be seen."

We quote this passage in order emphatically to point out the glorious realization of the prophecy herein set forth. In this mount—ran the saying—He shall be seen; "And when the fulness of the time was come," "When Solomon had made an end of praying, the fire came down from heaven, and consumed the burnt-offering and the sacrifices, and the glory of Jehovah filled the house. And the priests could not enter into the house of Jehovah, because the glory of Jehovah had filled Jehovah's house," 2 Chron. vii. 1, 2.

Later still, "A greater than Solomon is here," Matt. xii. 42. "It was revealed unto him (Simeon) by the Holy Ghost, that he should not see death before he had seen the Lord's Christ. And he came by the Spirit into the Temple, and when the parents brought in the child Jesus, to do for Him after the custom of the law, then took he Him up in his arms, and blessed God, and said, Lord, now lettest Thou thy servant depart in peace, according to thy word, for mine eyes have seen thy salvation," Luke ii. 26—30.

"CHAPTER X.

MOUNT GERIZIM THE MOUNT OF ABRAHAM'S SACRIFICE."

This chapter, being a continuation of the subject contained in the two previous chapters, need not occupy much time. The Bishop says:—" Hengstenberg's argument rests mainly on the assumption that the Mount Moriah which he supposes to be indicated in Gen. xxii. 2, is the same as that actually mentioned in the Hebrew text of 2 Chron. iii. 1, viz., the hill at Jerusalem on which the Temple was built, and where, as he imagines, the *second* appearance of Jehovah took place. But the fact is, that in only one single place of the Old Testament, viz., in the above passage in the Chronicles, written two hundred years after the captivity, is the name הַמּוֹרִיָּה, whatever may be its meaning, applied to the Temple hill at all.

" The following are some of the passages which prove, beyond a doubt, that the Temple, as well as the Tabernacle, was built on Mount Zion, Joel ii. 1, iii. 17; Obad. 17; Isa. viii. 8. In the following passages, Mount Zion is expressly distinguished from the whole city of Jerusalem, Joel ii. 32; Isa. x. 12, xxiv. 33. If the place of Abraham's sacrifice was really meant to point to Mount Moriah, on which the Temple was afterwards built, our confidence in the conjecture we have put forward, that Samuel was the Elohistic author of Genesis, would be shaken."

We are thus to consider two subjects—I. Was the Temple of Solomon built on Mount Moriah? II. Was Mount Gerizim the scene of Abraham's trial?

I. Was the Temple built on Mount Moriah?

As far as we know, there is but a single statement to this effect in God's Word; but in the absence of *proof* to the contrary, that must be held decisive. 2 Chron. iii. 1, thus states—

"Solomon began to build the house of the Lord in Mount Moriah, where the Lord appeared unto David his father, in the place that David had prepared in the threshing-floor of Ornan the Jebusite." We will now seek corroborative evidence.

At the very commencement of David's reign as king over all Israel, he resolved to make Jerusalem his capital; but the Upper City, or stronghold, was still held by the Jebusites; the Lower City occupying that portion of the holy site Josephus calls Acra. On Mount Zion stood the Jebusite fortress, which David needs must take; and Joab, his nephew, was the first Israelitish soldier to scale the defences of Zion. After the fortress was taken, great improvements were made upon the site, and it became known as the City of David. Josephus calls it the Upper City, to distinguish it from the Lower City, which covered a separate and lower hill (Acra), and was separated from that of Zion by a valley called in Scripture, Millo, but by Josephus, the Tyropœon. East of Acra, and north-east of Zion, was the Mount Moriah, on which the Temple was eventually built.

Now, we are told that David rebuilt the citadel upon Mount Zion, and erected thereon, by the assistance of Hiram, King of Tyre, a palace for his own residence; thus, with the dwelling-places around, and the tent for the Ark, wholly filling up the site of Zion. For David "stretched a tabernacle" for the Ark to rest upon Mount Zion, although the Tabernacle of Moses and the Levites remained at Gibeon. We thus see that Zion was fully occupied at the time Moriah was the threshing-floor of Ornan, or Araunah, the Jebusite. Further, when the Temple of Solomon was ready, we are informed, 1 Kings viii. 1, "Solomon assembled the elders of Israel and all the heads of the tribes, the chief of the fathers of the children of Israel, unto King Solomon in Jerusalem, *that they might bring up the Ark of the covenant of the Lord out of the City of David, which is Zion.*"

This is decisive, as, if the Temple had been built on Zion, there would have been no occasion to fetch the Ark *out of* the city of David, which is called Zion; and we thus have the statement of the Chronicler, that the Temple was built on Moriah, corroborated by the writer in 1 Kings, who states that it *was not* on Mount Zion. The Temple was indisputably built on the site of the threshing-floor of Araunah the Jebusite, which could not have occupied Mount Zion, because the Citadel, David's Palace, and the Tabernacle David had stretched for the Ark, were there; and concerning this threshing-floor, Josephus says: "Now it happened that Abraham came and offered his son Isaac for a burnt-offering *at that very place*," *Ant.*, b. vii. ch. xiii. 4.

We have thus a complete chain of evidence. The temple was built upon Mount Moriah, affirms the Chronicler; it was *not* built on Zion, witnesses the writer in the 1st book of Kings; that it was built on the threshing-floor of Araunah the Jebusite, all the witnesses agree; and at that very place, adds Josephus, Abraham came to offer his son Isaac.

We may also find the reason of so many references in the Psalms and Prophets to *Zion*, in the facts that the Ark was for a time located there; that the house of David was there; that the stronghold, which was the heart of the city, as the Temple was the glory of it, was there; and that for many years of its earlier history, "Jerusalem the holy" was built upon Mount Zion alone.

There is one error in the Bishop's statement that needs only pointing out, *i.e.*, that *the Tabernacle* was built upon Mount Zion. This appears to be a mistake through ignorance or carelessness. The Tabernacle was at Gibeon through all the reign of David, and until it was fetched from thence, and placed in the Temple by Solomon, 1 Kings viii. 3.

II. Was Mount Gerizim the scene of Abraham's trial?

Except it can be shown that the threshing-floor of Araunah

the *Jebusite*, was on Mount Gerizim, Josephus, as far as he can be considered an authority, settles the question in the negative. Nor do we know of a scintilla of evidence on the affirmative side of the question, except an assertion of Canon Stanley, as quoted by the Bishop; and the Samaritan tradition.

We give, here, the Samaritan tradition, quoted by Stanley, respecting Gerizim:—"Beyond all doubt (this is the form in which the story is told amongst the Samaritans themselves), Isaac was offered on Ar-Gerizim." Against this Samaritan tradition we may fairly balance the assertion of Josephus concerning the threshing-floor of Araunah, and thus far considering the external testimony equal, we have the Word of God asserting that Abraham's faith was tried, not on Mount Gerizim—there is no hint of the kind from beginning to end of the Holy Book—but on a mountain in the land of Moriah.

But as it may be thought that Canon Stanley's opinion, having been formed on the spot, is entitled to great weight, we shall quote on the opposite side the testimony of the Deputation from the Church of Scotland to the Jews in Palestine, in 1839:—"Turning to the west [they were standing on Mount Olivet], we looked down upon Jerusalem. We obtained a complete view of Mount Moriah, the hill nearest us, occupied by the Haram Sherif, or 'noble sanctuary,' with its Mahometan mosques. Here, probably, is the very hill where Abraham's uplifted hand was arrested when about to slay his son Isaac. Here the cry of David stayed the hand of the destroying angel. Here Solomon built the house of the Lord, where God dwelt between the cherubim."

So that McCheyne and Bonar arrived at a conclusion directly opposite to that of Canon Stanley; both opinions appearing to be formed on the spot itself.

We need not spend more time upon the matter. Bishop

Colenso's only reason for dwelling upon it is, that he imagines Moriah to be the only word in Genesis compounded with Jehovah; and we have demonstrated seven other instances of such compounding, and have shown also that the syllables forming the name יהוה are utterly unknown.

"CHAPTER XI.

THE NAMES ELOHIM AND JEHOVAH."

The Bishop thus writes:—"The word ELOHIM אֱלֹהִים is a plural noun; it is the general name for deity in the Hebrew language, and may be used accordingly for a heathen god. It is therefore quite a mistake to think of proving the doctrine of the Trinity, as some do, from the fact that Elohim is a *plural* name. Jehovah, however, is never used of a heathen god; it is the proper personal name of Him who is declared to be emphatically the covenant God of the Hebrew people. In Ex. iii. 14, אֶהְיֶה אֲשֶׁר אֶהְיֶה, 'I AM THAT I AM,' we find explained, apparently, the derivation of the name, יהוה, Jehovah,' according to the writer's view, from the Hebrew word היה, *hayah*, or הוה, *havah*, 'to be,' as if אהיה or אהוה, 'I AM,' were closely connected with יהוה, having at all events the same root with it. The proper vowel sounds of the word יהוה are indeed now unknown. It is difficult, however, to say what part of the verb הוה it can be, unless it be, as Gesenius and most German critics suppose (and so HENGSTENBERG, *Pent.* i. 247), a particular form of the future third pers. sing. יַהְוֶה *Jahveh*, or יַהֲוָה.

"This would agree with the Samaritan pronunciation as given

by Theodoret, *Quæst.* 15 *ad* Exod. vi., καλοῦσι δὲ αὐτὸ Σαμαρεῖται, ΙΑΒΕ, Ἰουδαῖοι δὲ ΑΙΑ, which last seems to point to אֶהְיֶה. But the ordinary form of the future of הוה is יִהְיֶה, as given in 1 Kings xiii. 32. The name ΙΑΩ, Diod. Sic. or ΙΑΟΥ, Clem. Alex., is evidently formed from the abbreviated Hebrew יָהוּ or יָהּ. Porphyry represents it by ΙΕΥΩ."

"Thus derived the name יהוה may be considered to mean HE IS, in opposition to the gods of the Gentiles, 'which are not,' which are 'no אֱלֹהִים,' Isa. xxxvii. 19, but mere אֱלִילִים 'vanities'; and to represent in the mouths of *men*, the 'self-existent Being,' the 'Eternal,' 'the living God,' 'Who was, and is, and is to come,' ὁ ὢν καὶ ὁ ἦν καὶ ὁ ἐρχόμενος, Rev. i. 8; whereas 'I Am' could only be properly used, as in Exod. iii. 14, by the Divine Being himself. Then, after this preparation in Exod. iii. 14, the word 'Jehovah' is used by the Elohist, as we believe for the first time, in v. 15."

Before entering into the consideration of the subject of this chapter, the names Elohim and Jehovah, it is only fair to point out—*that Bishop Colenso has taken the whole of the* STATEMENT *as above* (*without acknowledgment*) *from the Lexicon of Gesenius*. It is slightly, and very slightly, altered in the wording and arrangement, but it is so carelessly copied that in the copying from Theodoret (quoted by Gesenius) the word ΑΙΑ should be ΙΑΩ. (See Ges. Lex., p. 337.) We now pass to the consideration of the subject.

As the theory concerning the names Elohim and Jehovah is the basis of the whole argument contained in this Second Part, we shall at once enter into an extended consideration of it; and in order to do so systematically we must first inquire—If any reasons can be assigned why, in the inspired account of the creation of our world, in the introduction to the history of the intercourse between God and his human children, the word

אֱלֹהִים (Elohim: translated God in the English Bibles) should alone be used? And we answer—

I. That this name of the Deity is fittingly used as being the appellation of the One God most widely known amongst the nations of antiquity.

II. That this name of the Deity, from the ideas it conveyed to the minds of those acquainted with it, was the only appropriate one that could be used.

III. That in it is conveyed a germ of truth respecting the creation of the world, that no other name of the Deity known to a Hebrew could possibly convey.

I. That this name of the Deity is fittingly used as being the appellation of the One God most widely known amongst the nations of antiquity.

The Egyptians were a learned people for the times in which they lived; they were acquainted with many of the arts of our present civilization, e. g., weaving, smelting, refining, music, and astronomy. Moses was learned in all the knowledge of the Egyptians, who were in constant commercial intercourse with the nations that dwelt around them; consequently, many of them must have been acquainted with other languages beside their own; and, as Moses was learned in all their knowledge, doubtless the knowledge of languages was not neglected by him; if so, he would be competent to choose the name most appropriate for the occasion. Let us endeavour to ascertain if he did so.

The word used is אֱלֹהִים, derived from אֵל, prop. part. of the verb אוּל, signifying *strong, mighty;* and throughout the Hebrew scriptures it is applied (though not solely) to GOD himself. This Hebrew word אֵל is to be traced in other Shemitic dialects. Sanconiatho says: " Κατὰ τούτους γίνεταί τις Ἐλιοῦν

(עֶלְיוֹן) καλούμενος 'Ὕψιστος,' παραλαβὼν δὲ ὁ Οὐρανὸς τὴν τοῦ πατρὸς ἀρχὴν—ποιεῖται παῖδας δ' Ἴλον (אֵל ܠ̈ܐ) τὸν καὶ Κρόνον." Damascius (in Bochart) says also: "Φοίνικοὶ καὶ Σύροι τὸν Κρόνον Ἢλ καὶ Βὴλ καὶ Βολάθην (בֵּל אִיתן) ἐπονομάζουσιν," to which may be added, that in the apocryphal Sanconiatho, the allies of IL (אֵל), "'Ελοειμ ἐπεκλήθησαν," were called Eloïm. From "IL," or "Ilus," Cumberland (Orig. Gent. v. i., pp. 29 and 473) derives Ilium. The radical "EL" plays also a conspicuous part in Faber's "Cabiri," and in his "Pagan Idolatry," as also in Bryant's "Ancient Mythology" throughout, see especially v. i., p. 16 *seq.*: and p. 297, where חֹם־פִּי־אֵל " Hom-pi-el," the Oracle of Ham (the sun), is given as the etymology of Ὀμφαλὸν ἐριβρόμου χθονός while the same radicals, transposed, become אֵל־חֹם־פִּי " El-Hom-pi," Ὄλυμπος. In אֵל, too, we may probably look for the root of Ἥλιος, or Ἥέλιος, the first god worshipped by the heathen, Dius or Agni, the Sun. Sickler, (Cadmus, pp. 65, 104) derives Ἥλιος from הֲלִי־עֹז, and Ἥέλιος אִילִי־עֹז, which he translates, "the Power that gives light," and "the greatest Power." But the Syriac "Lib. Adami" says:

ܠܳܐ ܬܶܣܓܽܘܕܽܘܢ ܠܫܶܡܫܳܐ ܕܰܫܡܶܗ ܐܳܕܽܘܢܰܝ
ܕܰܫܡܶܗ ܩܳܕܽܘܫ ܐܰܝܠ ܐܰܝܠ ܫܡܶܗ

"Do not worship the Sun, whose name is Adonai (or Adoni), whose name is Kadusch (קָדֹשׁ, holy), whose name is EL, EL! (or IL, IL!)."

We find אֵל also preserved in Phœnician names, *e. g.*, "Cadmilus," the fourth Cabirus, who was of Phœnician extraction, is קַדְמִיאֵל "who stands before God."

We find it also amongst the Sabæans, Lib. Adami, pp. 294, 309, *seq.*: Hamam-il Hathm-il, and Nothr-il, and Zurz-il, and Pashr-il and Haltz-il.

It is in Ethiopic writings also, Lib. Enoch, c. vii. 9. And

these are the names of their angels: Samyūza, who is the chief of them, Urākibarme-el, Thami-el, Rāmu-el, Dān-el, etc.

Lastly, in Arabic we find also "Ilun," as a name for "God."

II. That this name of the Deity, from the *ideas it conveyed* to the minds of those acquainted with it, was the only appropriate one that could be used.

The one leading idea in אֵל, is that of *power*, and therefore of *pre-eminence*. God is called אֵל EL, as being THE MIGHTY, THE ONE ABOVE ALL, THE FIRST. From that idea of *power* and *excellence* grows, as a matter of course, the feeling of *awe*, which power inspires, and which leads men to *respect* and to *worship* it. Thus from אֵל, "God," comes אָלָה, to swear by God, and probably, also, אָלָה which, although not found in Hebrew as a root, is of frequent occurrence in Arabic اَلَّ and تَاَلَّ to "worship," to "serve," whence الاَهة and الِهة "worship"; and اَلَّ to "stand in awe"; from whence some derive الاِه "ILAHOUN,"

אֱלָהּ, "ELOAH," "GOD." He is called thus, they say, لانّه مألوه, because "He is feared and worshipped."

The same idea of *power* and supremacy are conveyed in the Chaldee אֱלָהּ "ELAH," from whence אֱלָהִי "divine," etc. In Syriac and Sabæan, "ALOHO," "GOD," from whence "alah," to "reckon as God." In Samar. "ALAH," "God." In Arabic, "Ilahoun," or "ILAH," "God."

Thus in every one of these ancient languages, the idea of the power or supremacy necessary to create a world is found in the word אֵל (which, as Gesenius remarks, is *a primitive word also*), and in no other word that we are aware of.

III. That in the word אֱלֹהִים, a germ of truth is conveyed

respecting the creation of the world; that no other name known to a Hebrew could possibly convey.

The word אֱלֹהִים is *plural*, though often used in a singular sense for THE ONE GOD—GOD. The Jewish rabbins say of it in this sense that it is the "pluralis majestaticus vel excellentiæ," the plural of powers or virtues, which is used in expressions of sovereignty. Aben Ezra is of this opinion, when he says: "After that we have found אֱלוֹהַּ we know that אֱלֹהִים is the plural thereof, and the origin of the use of it, is according to the genius of the language; for every tongue has it own honorific terms;—and, in the 'holy tongue' the way to express 'honour,' as, for instance, to a superior, is to use the plural, as in Lords for Lord, Masters for Master, etc."

But the Christian who believes in the Divinity of the Lord Jesus Christ, and the Personality of the Holy Spirit, will not fail to see in this word—dimly shadowed from the very foundation of the world, expressed in the very commencement of Revelation— the names of the Father, Son, and Holy Spirit. He will remember the testimony of the beloved disciple, "There are three that bear record in heaven." He will remember the witness of the Apostle Paul, " God .. hath in these last days spoken unto us by his Son, whom He hath appointed heir of all things, *by whom also He made the worlds*," and he will thankfully recognize the reason why,—and exult in the knowledge that, in the very first verse of the first chapter of the Holy Book, there is a shadowing out of the Lord Jesus in the name of the ONE GOD; and from this first dim glimpse of Him, He is revealed more and more, in brighter and clearer light, until "the Desire of all nations" came. And this name, אֱלֹהִים will remain an unalterable witness to all nations, until He shall " appear the second time without sin unto salvation."

We thus see that the word which has been chosen to introduce the idea of the Almighty God in the Revelation of his will to the creatures He has made, is the one best known to the ancient Heathen world, that it is satisfactory to the Jew, and full of hope and promise to the Christian; and if our eyes are opened thus to see Him "whom to know is life eternal," and we rejoice in his light, let us praise Him for so great a benefit, and say with Djelāl-ed-din (Diwan, p. 210, ed Rosenzw.) :—

از تو لبحقّ رسيده ام اي حقّ حقّ كذار من
شكر ترا ستاده ام شمس من خداي من

"Through Thee alone I have attained to Truth, O Thou TRUTH itself! Thou hast imparted it to me! And here I stand to thank Thee, Lord! mine only Sun and my God!"

Having thus seen at length the meaning of the word אֱלֹהִים (ELOHIM), supposed by the Bishop to indicate the writer called the Elohist, we shall now endeavour to ascertain the meaning of the name יְהֹוָה (JEHOVAH), supposed by the Bishop to indicate a second writer, called the Jehovist. In doing this, we shall endeavour to show that there is good reason why these different names should be used as they are used by Moses in the Pentateuch, and by other writers in the later portions of God's Word.

We shall first gather up from Jewish sources of high authority, the recognized meaning of the word, as set forth by Jewish writers of acknowledged eminence; and secondly, present the explanation of the word as it is given by Christian authors.

In the Talmud, tr. שבועות ch. שבועת העדות we read, "The names (of the Deity) which it is forbidden to erase, are, the most holy name of the four letters, יהוה, El, Elohim, Eloha, Adonai, Ehyeh, Shaddai, Tsebaoth." Although there are thus several names assigned to the Deity, there are two particularly distinguished, and of more frequent occurrence in the Holy Scriptures, than any of the others. These are Jehovah, the

Lord, and Elohim, God. Their particular distinction consists in the following points:—

1. Whenever the Deity reveals Himself to a prophet, or when any prophet addresses the Deity, we never find, throughout the whole of the scriptures, any other name used than one of these two, or both.

2. These two names, when joined, often change places; as sometimes the expression is, *The Lord God*, and sometimes *God the Lord*. Of the first, out of many instances, we quote Deut. iii. 24, "O Lord God thou hast begun to shew thy servant thy greatness," &c.; and of the second, Hab. iii. 19, "God the Lord is my strength." Such transpositions do not occur in any other name of the Deity.

3. No adjective or other designation ever precedes these two names; thus, for instance, we never in the Scriptures find "Tsebaoth the Lord," but always find The Lord Tsebaoth; nor merciful Lord, but the Lord, merciful, &c.

4. The name JEHOVAH is never in regimen except by means of the names ELOHIM or EL, God, joined to it, as, THE LORD God of hosts, the Lord God of Israel, etc.

5. JEHOVAH is sometimes punctuated with the same vowel-points as ELOHIM, and is read accordingly; but ELOHIM is never punctuated with the vowel-points proper to Jehovah, which, in fact, are not known to us.

To understand these peculiarities, it is necessary to know the following points:—JEHOVAH denotes God in the abstract idea, as He cannot be understood by the human mind; and applies solely to his own Being, without any relative connection whatever. Accordingly the Rabbins expound the text, "They shall pronounce my name over the children of Israel," Num. vi. 27. "*My name*, the name which relates solely to Me;" consequently this name has no relation to any being, but to Himself alone.

Elohim denotes the emanation of every good which brings the Deity into any relation with his creatures and his creative power, which gave existence to all that *is*.

Accordingly, this name only (Elohim) is used in the history of the creation; and whenever the powers of creation, as evinced in nature, are mentioned by any of the sacred writers, this name only is used, from its being in direct connection with the act of creation. Consequently, whenever the prevailing idea of the Sacred Writer is the Deity in the abstract, Jehovah is placed before Elohim; but when the prevailing idea refers to the powers of creation, Elohim precedes Jehovah.

For these reasons no adjective can ever precede these names, because such cannot be applied to the Deity in the abstract; nor can an adjective follow Jehovah, except by means of Elohim, as it is only in consequence of the creation that God's creatures can append any attribute to his name.

Thence, likewise, Jehovah is sometimes punctuated with the vowel points of Elohim, but the reverse can never be; for although we may, from the emanations of his Omnipotence, become conscious of his abstract Being, yet we cannot conceive how the creative powers could emanate from that Being, who is altogether abstract and above our comprehension.

As the name Elohim thus expresses the relation between the creative power that bestows and the creatures that receive, it is in the Hebrew, applied to those created beings also, who, in virtue of their official situation, bestow on others who receive. Thence angels are called Elohim, as they are the Divine instruments to bestow God's bounties on the world. Thence, too, was that name applied to idols, as their worshippers held them to be the dispensers of everything. This designation is also extended to judges or rulers who dispense justice to their inferiors. But whenever thus applied, the word Elohim is always plural;

whereas, when limited to its original purpose, that of expressing the proper name of the Deity, it is always singular. (Though, as we have shown previously, there is also an intimation of the Three in One in this name.)

We now quote two well-known writers in support of this view.

Abarbanel says: "The plural termination, ים, *im*, does not affect this noun proper any more than it does Ephra-im or Mitzra-im, proper names, which, though terminating in *im*, are nevertheless singular" (but may we not add, "There are Three that bear record in heaven, and these Three are One ?"). And Sir Isaac Newton says: "The Most High God is a Being, eternal, infinite, absolutely perfect (יְהֹוָה); but a being, however perfect, without dominion, is not God the Ruler. *The word* GOD *always signifies* RULER (אֱלֹהִים); but every Ruler is not God. The rule of a spiritual being makes him God; true rule, a true God; the highest rule, the highest God; feigned rule, feigned God."

Having thus shown the Jewish idea of the name Jehovah, we shall conclude this subject by appending some thoughts from the Hebrew Lexicon that are attributed to Professor Lee, appertaining to the word יְהֹוָה, as concerning the Lord Jesus Christ.

That, אֶהְיֶה אֲשֶׁר אֶהְיֶה, "I AM THAT I AM," has reference to this term, I think there can be no doubt; and that Rev. i. 4—8, ὁ ὢν καὶ ὁ ἦν καὶ ὁ ἐρχόμενος, refers to it likewise, is perhaps equally certain. But these relate to its interpretation, not to its form, nor to its pronunciation; and as this is manifestly the most important part of the inquiry, let us see what can be deduced from it.

"It is quite certain, then, that the latter place in the Apocalypse applies to Christ; comp. vers. 7, 8, 17, 18. A similar passage occurs Heb. xiii. 8. Both these, therefore, cannot but refer to Christ. Again. reference—Rev. i. 17—is certainly made to Isa. xli. 4; and there יְהֹוָה is the person designated the *First*, etc.; and in truth the theology of the Hebrews will admit of this term being applied to no other. From an extended inquiry, instituted on comparisons of this sort, the most irrefragable proofs of the divinity of Christ might be collected; and it will be found eventually that it is quite impossible to understand innumerable passages of the Old Testament on any other view.

"Now, the spirit of the Scriptures goes principally to the point of a *revealed, manifested,* and *known God;* not to a mere theoretical or metaphysically-imagined deity; and as the term, אֱלֹהִים (Elohim), had, before the time of Moses (Gen. xxxi. 30, etc.), been applied to idols, the representatives of these metaphysical nonentities, it seems to me that the terms אֶהְיֶה and יִהְיֶה, more particularly the latter, were chosen in order to keep up this marked and very important distinction; and, above all, to keep up the memorial of his promised manifestation in the flesh. Comp. Isa. vii. 14, with Obad. ix. 5, 6, and Mic. v. 2—4, which was apparently had in view in the passages cited above from the Epistle to the Hebrews, the Revelation of St. John, etc.; and to show that in Jesus of Nazareth the person named יְהֹוָה in the Old Testament was manifested to the world."—Heb. and Chal. Lex. p. 249.

Thus seen in the various lights in which we have endeavoured to place them, these names of the Deity—Elohim and Jehovah—are full of instruction and strength, and comfort and hope. While in the Jewish teaching there is the dim outreach after Him " whom no man hath seen nor can see," "the Father of an Infinite Majesty," " God over all, blessed for evermore;" there is in the Christian thought, " God manifest in the flesh."

"Without controversy, great is the mystery of godliness;" "Now we see through a glass, darkly, but then face to face," with "Him who only hath immortality, dwelling in the light which no man can approach unto, whom no man hath seen nor can see, to whom be honour and power everlasting. Amen."

"CHAPTERS XII.—XVIII.

THE ELOHISTIC AND JEHOVISTIC PSALMS CONSIDERED."

WITH a very few general remarks, we may pass the whole of this part of the Bishop's book, the value of the theme being plainly exhibited in the following quotation from the Bishop's Introduction to it:—" Let us examine, then, for this [Elohistic and Jehovistic] purpose, the Book of Psalms, and those Psalms especially, in the first instance, which appear by their titles to have been written in the earlier part of David's life. And let us see if David makes use of the name Jehovah, as freely as *we should expect him* to use it from what we find in the Pentateuch,—as freely as he *must* have used it, if the word was in common use in his days, and believed to have had set upon it the seal, as it were, of Jehovah Himself, as the name by which He would be known as the Covenant God of Israel."

We do not see that we can touch this without spoiling it altogether; for a specimen of conceited arrogance, it is surely unexampled in the history of criticism. It makes our expectation the arbiter, our sense of fitness the test, of what Divine Truth ought to be; and unless the Psalm reaches that standard, it must be rejected.

But this is a world wherein there are such things as differences of opinion; one man may be satisfied with one hundredth part of that which is required to satisfy another; and, consequently, if we are to have a standard at all, we needs must elect some one to whom all other men shall bow, some one whose expectations and sense of fitness shall be final. But inasmuch as there may be some little difficulty and delay in obtaining the universal and concurrent opinion as to who this shall be; we may be excused from spending more time on the question at present.

Our next extract is a specimen of the manner in which critics agree on the question of the date of the Psalms, which, be it remembered, is a necessary preliminary to entering into Elohistic and Jehovistic theories. Thus, Bishop Colenso writes concerning the 51st Psalm: "Dr. Davidson says the *beginning* of the Babylonish captivity is the probable date." "Hengstenberg writes that the Psalm was composed by David on the occasion of his sin with Bathsheba." "Ewald assigns this Psalm to some time after the destruction of the Temple." "Olshausen to the times of the Maccabees." Hupfeld writes, "The Psalm must belong to the time after the Babylonish captivity;" and the Bishop sums up by gravely adding, "The above reasoning, however, does not appear to me to be convincing."

There is a point worth notice in the remarks on the sixty-eighth Psalm. The Bishop states: "We may recur with confidence to the usual supposition which connects it with the removal of the Ark, in David's time, to Mount Zion."

Here, then, the Bishop allows we have a distinct and truthful historical allusion, freely admitted to be correct in date and detail; so that we may start from this point as one of mutual agreement. The removal of the Ark from Kirjath-Jearim to Zion took place about ten years after David became king. It had remained at Kirjath-Jearim twenty years, had been one year in the hands of the Philistines, and was previously under the care of Eli, in the Tabernacle at Shiloh, for many years. This brings us to a period before Samuel was born, and it is certain that when Samuel was brought—a little child—to be with Eli at Shiloh, the Ark was there before him; consequently, its origin and presence there have to be accounted for. Upon the supposition of the historical truth of the Mosaic Narrative, we are perfectly acquainted with both. But taking up the other question, upon the supposition that Samuel wrote the Pentateuch, we ask for an account of the origin of the Ark that shall explain the joy of the people at its removal, and shall harmonize with the Narrative that the Bishop allows to be historically true.

It being also certain that both the Ark and the Tabernacle were made before Samuel was born, we call upon the Bishop to account for their origin and connection with each other on the supposition that Samuel wrote the Pentateuch.

"CHAPTER XIX.

THE JEHOVISTIC NAMES IN THE BOOK OF JUDGES."

The Bishop thus states his case:—" From the doubt which exists as to the proper vowel-sounds, with which this Name (Jehovah) should be enunciated, it has been suggested that it may be, perhaps, a word of foreign origin; cognate, perhaps, with the Sanscrit Dyaus, from which is derived the Greek, Ζεύς, Διος, and the Latin, Ju, which appears in Ju-piter, Jov-is; and that this word may have been adopted among the Hebrews, being first corrupted into the form יהו, yehu, and so referred to the Hebrew root, יָהָ. In fact, one very common form of the name is יָהּ, yah, or יָהוּ, yahu. One strong objection to this theory appears to be in the fact that the Sanscrit word, and its derivations, have all an initial sound of *d*, which the Hebrew has not. But however this may be, whether the word Jehovah be a corruption of a foreign word, or originated by some great authority among the Hebrews themselves, it must have been gradually brought into popular use, doubtless in a great measure by means of such Psalms as these."

The Bishop then quotes from Hengstenberg as follows:—
"*Unless persons pronounce* (which few will venture to do) *the Pentateuch in all its parts to be spurious*, so that no inference can be be drawn from it respecting the state of the language in the time of Moses, *they will be forced to carry back the formation and introduction of the name beyond the Mosaic age*, from which another important consequence will follow, that the idea of the Israelitish national God cannot be the fundamental idea."

Before proceeding further with the Bishop's ideas, we will remark upon those above quoted, the last first.

We have never seen Hengstenberg's book, and were utterly in ignorance of his words as above quoted; but to compare great things with small, it will be seen how strikingly the view of the great critic has been confirmed by the independent researches of two mechanics. It will be remembered that we have shown first that there is *no reason why* we should not carry back the formation of the name beyond the Mosaic age, by showing that the passage in Exod. vi. 3, "By my name Jehovah was I not known to them," is not a statement made, but a question put to Moses; and, secondly, by exhibiting eight instances of actual compounding with Jehovah in names taken from the pre-Mosaic period; in one of these from before the Flood.

And further, in the name of the first created woman חוה (Eve), the last half of the name יהוה is identical with the termination of her name. Whether these simple facts have escaped the notice of all the German critics, we do not know, but there are the names as plain (to any one accustomed to the use of Hebrew *as a language*) as any simple word of English letters to an educated Englishman. We now pass backward to the Bishop's own words,—that is to say, as far as they are his, and not borrowed without acknowledgment from previous authors. The ideas concerning the name of Jehovah being taken from the Latin

Ju-piter and Jov-is are found in the Lexicon of Gesenius (p. 337), where the statement is thus printed:—" I suppose the word to be one, of the most remote antiquity, perhaps of the same origin as *Jovis Jupiter.*"

It is to be remarked that Bishop Colenso adopts these opinions; and, *for the present*, abides by them; but Gesenius afterward THOROUGHLY retracted them, see Thes. and Amer. trans. in voc., where he calls such comparisons and derivations " waste of time and labour."

That Bishop Colenso has copied these remarks from other authors, without being aware of the utterly destructive manner in which they can be brought to bear upon the Jehovistic theory he is advocating, we shall prove to demonstration in the commencement of the next chapter, to which we now refer our readers.

One other remark and we pass on. The Bishop states: " From the *doubt which exists as to the proper vowel sounds*, with which this name should be enunciated, it has been suggested that it may be perhaps a word of foreign origin."

When it has been necessary to show by syllabic forms of names the non-compounding with the name Jehovah, the Bishop carefully kept back this knowledge (if he had it) from the reader, and with good reason, for *his whole theory, from beginning to end, is based upon vowel-sounds, which he here confesses are unknown;* and even after this admission he continues to harp upon the *syllabic compounds* with the name Jehovah, while *the whole name in its contracted forms*, as compounded with names of persons, has entirely escaped his notice, though it is fatal as regards his theory.

We have now to consider the Jehovistic names in the book of Judges, which Bishop Colenso has pointed out as being there, and has endeavoured to account for. We shall afterward point out two that he has not mentioned, through evident ignorance of their existence as Jehovistic names. The names quoted by the Bishop are Joash, Jotham, Micah, and Jonathan; with Joshua and Jochebed introduced from the Pentateuch; and we will now see the manner in which he disposes of these six instances.

"If Joash here be the same as Jehoash, it would of course be compounded with Jehovah. But the name יוֹאָשׁ, Joash, may have been derived from יָאַשׁ as יוֹסֵף, Joseph, from יָסַף. In like manner יוֹתָם, Jotham, may be derived from the old form, יָתֹם =יָמַם." (Gesen. Lex.) "So too, Micah, which is considered by some to be an abridged form of Micaiah, 'Who is like Jehovah,' is by others distinguished from the latter name, and explained to mean 'poor,' or 'smitten,' or 'who is here?'"

It cannot surely be possible that Bishop Colenso ever thought of having enemies of his theory to convert into friends, or he surely would not have exhibited such weakness as he has thus displayed. Put into plain language, the case stands thus: To support Bishop Colenso's theory, there should be no Jehovistic names in the Book of Judges; but here are three indisputable names which break up the theory, therefore something must be done to get rid of them. Consequently the Bishop suggests that they *may mean something else.* It is true they *may*, but *do* they? They are in all copies, there is no charge of interpolation brought; the weak suggestion is made that they *may not be* what *they are*, and they are first quietly shelved, and afterward ignored. But is it unreasonable to ask for something stronger than a suggestion that what *is* one thing *may be* another, before we part with our Bibles?

"There can be no doubt," continues the Bishop, "that Jonathan is compounded with Jehovah, and means, 'Jehovah gives.' If we could be reasonably certain that this was a *bona fide* historical name, and that a man, called Jonathan, was actually priest to the tribe of Dan (Jud. xviii. 30), *before* the time of Samuel, it would follow, of course, that the name Jehovah was not first *introduced* by Samuel. But then we are met by the fact that this is the *only* name in the whole history of the Judges, with respect to which it can be confidently maintained that it is compounded with Jehovah." " In the English Version, Jud. xviii. 30, he is said to be the son of Gershom, the son of Manasseh. This is the reading of the text in the Hebrew Bible, but the more approved marginal reading has מֹשֶׁה, Moses, instead of מְנַשֶּׁה, and the *vulgate* adopts this reading, which, says Bleek, is '*certainly correct*,' and, according to Kuenen, 'is now generally adopted.' According to this, Jonathan was apparently the grandson of Moses."

Now let us see what answer the Bishop gives to this strong argument as stated by himself. His reply to it is simply a charge of interpolation. Since the name cannot be expunged, it is said to be interpolated. But a more unfortunate word against which to bring a charge of interpolation could scarcely be found. The Bishop says the text in the Hebrew Bible reads Manasseh, but this is simply untrue. We have examined many different editions of the Hebrew Bible, *and in every one of them the interpolation* of the נ is distinctly marked by being placed in a different position from the letters of the text. If the Jews, then, would not alter the text so much as by a letter, even to remove so deep a stain from the family of Moses, as that of his grandson being the first idolatrous priest; it is not conceivable that, unless for the same strong reason, they would have allowed the name of Jonathan to remain at all. In fact it must be seen at a glance that no other reason than *the integrity of the text* can be assigned for the retention of the name of Jonathan. If ancient Jews had believed the passage in which it occurs to be an interpolation, they would have removed it many centuries since. And the very fact of the name being found in the text (with such pressing reasons for its excision in existence) is proof of its integrity as strong as need be desired.

Having thus disposed of these four troublesome names, the Bishop proceeds: " Upon the whole, then, we conclude that there is no single instance in the authentic history, from the time of Moses downward to that of Samuel, which can be appealed to as distinctly showing that the name Jehovah was used in the formation of proper names in those days, except, as before, the cases of Joshua and Jochebed." " The Elohist himself makes the change of Hoshea to Jehoshua in a very marked manner, and (concerning Jochebed) it seems very strange that if the names of the father and mother of Moses were known to the writer of the account of his birth in Ex. ii., they should not have been mentioned at the first, instead of its being stated quite vaguely; 'There went a man of the house of Levi and took to wife a daughter of Levi.' "

And this is the *proof* we are offered concerning the Jehovistic names of Joshua and Jochebed; in the one case, *the name was changed suddenly*, in the other, *if it was known it was strange it was not mentioned before!* To comment upon this would be more time lost in addition to that already wasted in reading and copying it.

And now, how stands the case of the six names mentioned by the Bishop? Three, he informs us, *may be* something else, and three are said to be *interpolated*. But not an atom of proof is given in any one case against the integrity of the text. But since these names do not please the Bishop as Jehovistic, we will offer two more for his consideration. The first is the name Jair (before mentioned), which occurs again, Jud. x. 3—5, in which case the name of Jehovah is represented by the ׳ being doubted; the second is that of Jabin, king of Hazor, the meaning of whose name is "whom Jehovah considered" (see Ges. Lex. p. 327). How this name came into the possession of a heathen prince, we do not pretend to explain; but it is found in Josh. xi. 1 and Jud. iv. 2. And that it is there found is sufficient to overthrow Bishop Colenso's assertion, even allowing (which it is seen we do not) that he has explained away those instances quoted by himself.

There is one other remark before quitting this chapter. We have seen that the principal part of the Jehovistic ideas in this second portion of Dr. Colenso's work are taken from the articles on that subject in the lexicon of Gesenius. We shall now see that Gesenius is responsible for some part of Dr. Colenso's new belief. The Bishop writes as follows:—"My own conviction, however, from the accumulated evidence (!) of various kinds before us is, that Samuel was the first to form and introduce the name, perhaps in imitation of *some Egyptian name of the Deity which may have reached his ears.*" Gesenius wrote before him: "I suppose this word to be one of the most remote antiquity, perhaps of the same origin as *Jovis, Jupiter,* and *transferred from the Egyptians to the Hebrews*" (see Lex. p. 337).

This opinion, as we have shown, Gesenius afterward thoroughly retracted, probably through having become convinced that the Egyptian Gems on which it was founded were the work of heretics of the second and third centuries. Bishop Colenso, however, adopts the discarded opinion of Gesenius, and parades it as his own. We think he might at least have had the candour to acknowledge from whence it was obtained.

"CHAPTER XX.

THE JEHOVISTIC NAMES IN THE BOOK OF SAMUEL."

The Bishop thus writes :—" We now pass on to the First Book of Samuel. Here, throughout the first chapters, we do not meet with a single name compounded with Jehovah, though we find *El*kanah and *El*ihu, i. 1; *El*i, i. 9; Samu*el*, ii. 18; *El*eazar, vii. 1."

From this brief extract we will take *one single word*, and with it prove—

I. That Bishop Colenso does not understand Hebrew.

II. That it completely explodes the Elohistic and Jehovistic theory.

III. That Samuel did not first form and introduce the name Jehovah.

The word that will do all this is the name Elihu.

I. The name Elihu will prove that Bishop Colenso does not understand Hebrew.

The meaning of the name Elihu, in Hebrew, is exactly the same as Elijah, Jehovah—He is God; or to transpose it in Hebrew as it stands in English, God—He is Jehovah. With this word, *written by himself in the same sentence*, nothing but gross ignorance of the Hebrew language could have made Dr. Colenso fall into the mistake of asserting "throughout the first chapters we do not meet with a single name compounded with Jehovah."

Further, it proves ignorance of the meaning of the words *he has copied from the lexicon*, and inserted in the commencement of Chapter XIX., for there the reader will find quoted, the Hebrew word that forms the last and largest portion of the name Elihu (יהו), and this Hebrew word is there expressly stated to be a contraction of the name Jehovah.

In his page 331 Bishop Colenso *copies:* "In fact one very common form of the name Jehovah is יָהּ, yah, or יָהוּ, yahu."

In p. 344 he asserts: "We do not meet with a single name compounded with Jehovah, though we find Elkanah and Elihu."

Now, Elihu in Hebrew is written thus, אֱלִיהוּא, and it will be seen at a glance that the Bishop's own copying of the contraction for Jehovah, יהו, yahu, is there. We think this is certain proof that the Bishop does not understand Hebrew, for it seems impossible to believe that any one, *who understood what he was writing,* would have penned two sentences diametrically opposed to each other, such as those above quoted.

But there is another proof of the Bishop's ignorance of Hebrew *in the same sentence*, shown in his asserting the name of *Eli* to be compounded with *Elohim:* because it has *El* in English, he has taken for granted that it is the same in Hebrew, but it is not so; the name of the high priest, Eli עֵלִי means "going up," perhaps "height," (Ges. Lex., p. 632), whereas the word that is compounded with *El*ohim is אֱלִי, "my God!" (Ges. Lex., p. 45). If the Bishop has any knowledge of Hebrew, he must be aware that the letter ע which commences the name of Eli in Hebrew is never used to form part of the Divine name, the letter that is invariably employed for that purpose is א, the first letter of the Hebrew alphabet.

II. This word—Elihu—completely explodes the Elohistic and Jehovistic theory; it is indisputable that this name, written in full, would be *El*-Jehovah, therefore it contains within itself both the Elohistic and Jehovistic names of the Deity. The Jewish authorities assert that this name rightly spelled in the Hebrew contains the whole of the Divine name, thus אלי־יהוה; but inasmuch as this name is never, *as a whole,* conferred upon any human being, they take away the final ה, and substitute the א; so, indeed, destroying the full identity, yet leaving in the name the contracted form of Jehovah set forth by Dr. Colenso. Now Bishop Colenso asserts, and the whole theory of his book is founded upon the assertion, that the Elohist, Samuel, was the older writer, and that the Jehovistic writer came afterward. Here, then, is a word containing both Elohim and Jehovah, indisputably in existence for four generations before the oldest of these two writers was born.

III. This name, Elihu, will prove that Samuel did not "first form and introduce the name" Jehovah.

Elihu was Samuel's great-grandfather, and as the name of Elihu contains the whole of the name Jehovah, it was *absolutely impossible* that his great-grandson, Samuel, could have "first formed and introduced the name."

To make good his assertion that Samuel "first formed and introduced the name" Jehovah; Bishop Colenso must prove that Samuel "first formed and introduced the name" of his own great grandfather!

Here, then, is Bishop Colenso's whole theory, laid by himself in utter and irremediable ruin. That Samuel "first formed and introduced the name Jehovah" is shown to be ridiculously impossible, as it was the name conferred upon and commonly used by his own great grandfather. The fact that he had it, indisputably carries us back to his parents; and, so far, back into the times of the judges of Israel; and this instance, coupled with the others that have been mentioned, form an unbroken chain of Jehovistic names from Eve down to the times of Samuel himself.

With this chapter the Bishop ends, for the present, his Criticism on the Word of God, and to have more signally failed in proving his case, or to have concluded with an argument more disgracefully and glaringly absurd, would have been impossible.

"CHAPTER XXI.

SUMMARY OF RESULTS IN PART II."

We have but little space left, and therefore must very rapidly pass over this and the concluding chapter of the Bishop's present Part. He promises, however, to make Part III. as intelligible as possible to the reader who does not understand Hebrew—thereby at least insinuating that he himself is a profound Hebraist. If so, he has a most unhappy way of convincing Jews that he understands their form of speech; for they assert that any intelligent lad with a knowledge of the Alphabet, a Hebrew Lexicon, Grammar, and a copy of the Hebrew Scriptures, would be able to detect the Bishop's palpable blunders. But we must hasten to notice the more prominent points of the summary in question.

I. " There are different authors concerned in the composition of the Book of Genesis, whose accounts, in some respects, contradict each other."

So Tom Paine asserted before Bishop Colenso. We have seen that Bishop Watson has succesfully defended the Bible against both attacks.

V. " If the name Jehovah *was* first revealed to Moses (in Exod. vi.) then the Jehovistic story which puts it in the mouths of persons of all classes from the days of Eve downwards, cannot be historically true."

We have shown that it is *not* asserted in Ex. vi. 3, that the name Jehovah was then first revealed on the earth—the words form a question, not a statement of a fact; and there is good reason to believe that the name of Eve herself is in the last portion compounded with the name Jehovah.

VI. " In the Book of Genesis, down to the age of Joseph,

though there are numerous names compounded with Elohim, *there is not a single one compounded with Jehovah."*

No one acquainted with the Hebrew language would venture upon the assertion. There is Eve, Mehujael, Judah, Joseph, Jemuel, Jamin, and Jachin—all compounded with Jehovah, though Bishop Colenso's critical ability has failed to detect the facts.

VIII., IX., X., and XI. " We must return, then, to the other supposition, viz., that the Elohist had some special reason for commending the name to the regard and veneration of the people. The most natural reason would be that he himself was introducing it, as a new name for the God of Israel. We find an indication of the fact that the name did not exist before the time of SAMUEL, in the circumstance that *throughout the history in the book of Judges there is no single name which can be appealed to with confidence as compounded with Jehovah,* while there are names compounded with the divine name in the form of EL. . . . . During and after the time of Samuel we observe a gradually increasing partiality for the use of names compounded with Jehovah, while not one name of this kind occurs at such an age as is inconsistent with the supposition that this name may have been introduced by Samuel."

In the book of Judges there are the Jehovistic names of Joash, Jotham, Micah, Joshua, Jonathan, Jair, and Jabin, and if "not one name of this kind occurs at such an age as is inconsistent with the supposition that this name may have been introduced by Samuel," it is indisputable that Samuel must have "introduced the name of *his own great grandfather,* Elihu."

XIV. " We conclude, then, with some degree of confidence, that Samuel was the Elohistic writer of the Pentateuch."

And, therefore, that he invented the name of his own great grandfather, the history of the Ark of the Covenant, and of the Tabernacle of the Congregation *that were in Shiloh before he was born.* And it is certain that the Tabernacle and its accessories were worth about two hundred and fifty thousand pounds, but we must suppose, in order to accept Bishop Colenso's theory, that the Israelites were in actual possession of this valuable property, without having the least idea how they came by it.

XV. "Since the Jehovistic writer makes free use of the name Jehovah, he must have written later than the early days of David."

It remains to be shown that the name was not known in Paradise, and that the name of Eve is not compounded with it, and we have shown that in the name of Mehujael the compounding with the name Jehovah certainly occurred in antediluvian periods.

XVI. "This is confirmed by finding that one Jehovistic passage, Num. x. 35, is manifestly copied from a Psalm of David."

This is begging the whole question; there is not any valid reason given to prove that the portion of the Psalm has not been copied from Numbers.

XX. "The book of Deuteronomy was written about the time of Josiah, and, as some supposed, by the hand of the Prophet Jeremiah."

If so, Jeremiah wrote the book of Deuteronomy on the plains of Moab, and delivered it to the Levites to keep, before the Israelites passed over Jordan, *about eight hundred years before he was born.* (See Deut. xxxi. 24—26.)

"CHAPTER XXII.

CONCLUDING REMARKS."

The Bishop thus writes :—" I must now, in conclusion, take account of two classes of objections, which will undoubtedly be made to the above result. First, it will be said, 'You will have us, then, believe that Samuel, Nathan, etc., were after all *deceivers*, who palmed upon their own countrymen in the first instance a gross fraud, which from that time to this has been believed to be the true word of the living God.' As one of my own friends has observed, I would rather believe that two and two make five, than that such a man as SAMUEL could possibly have been guilty of so foul an offence against the laws of religious truth and common morality. I answer in the first place, that for any one who is ready to believe that two and two make five, if he finds it written down in the Bible, there is, as it seems to me, no alternative but to comply with this demand of a merely superstitious reverence for the outward letter, the husk of the Bible, and abrogate the rights and duties of a reasoning being; for, undoubtedly, as I have shown, I believe sufficiently in Part I., an unquestioning and implicit faith in all the details of the story of the Exodus, as recorded in the Pentateuch, involves, again and again, assent to propositions as monstrous and absurd as the above statement would be in arithmetic."

Let us see what this verbiage amounts to. "Any one who is ready to believe that two and two make five, if he finds it in the Bible, must abrogate the rights and duties of a reasoning being." Exactly so, we fully admit the inference drawn; but does the Bible anywhere state that two and two make five? If not, why introduce such stuff to distract the reader's attention? Or does the Bible anywhere state or hint that Samuel wrote the Pentateuch, or even a single line, or a word of it? If not, how is the Bible concerned, in any way, on either side of the question at issue?

But a man who believes that two and two make five must "abrogate the rights and duties of a reasoning being." We do not think more faith is required to swallow "this monstrous and absurd proposition," than to believe Dr. Colenso's theory; *for it is as easy to believe that two and two make five as to believe that Samuel "first formed the name of—his own great-grandfather!"*

"To others," Bishop Colenso continues, "I reply—It is not I who require you to abandon the ordinary notion of the Mosaic authorship and antiquity of the Pentateuch. It is the TRUTH itself which does so."

To this *we* reply by pointing out that we have demonstrated the *untruths* upon which Dr. Colenso's whole theory is founded. And, further, it is impossible that the TRUTH can require us to believe that any man ever wrote a book eight hundred years before he was born; but it *is* absolutely necessary to believe this, in order to receive the theory propounded by the Bishop of Natal.

We may mention three more theories we must receive in order to agree with Dr. Colenso.

Without a shadow of evidence of any kind, we must believe the prophet SAMUEL to be the most blasphemous and successful forger and liar the world ever saw.

We must believe the Jews of all ages to have been such monstrous fools as to have insisted upon retaining a forged book in their midst, which they had every opportunity of proving to be false, but which has, through all time, held them under burdens heavy and grievous to be borne.

We must believe, also, that the modern Jews do not understand their own language, for it is unquestionable, that *if* Dr. Colenso understands Hebrew, *the Jews do not.* (See Dr. Adler's letter to the "Athenæum.")

Of the whole matter, here is the sum:—

Jesus Christ the Son of God bore emphatic witness, many times repeated, that Moses wrote the Pentateuch.

This witness the Bishop of Natal declares to be false, when he asserts the Pentateuch to have been written by Samuel and later writers.

But in endeavouring to prove his assertion of the falsehood of our Lord's testimony, the Bishop of Natal has put forward some of the most monstrous and palpable absurdities, that ever rendered a man—who wished to be thought wise and learned—a common laughing stock.

Alas for us, to whom the revelation of the will of God has been given—

"The Word of our GOD is the source of peace, and brings peace to all. But we make war with it; with it we think of strife; with it we hate one another; and, again, with it we prepare destruction for ourselves."

THE END.

BS1225.4 .C7E3
The Bible in the workshop : a refutation
Princeton Theological Seminary-Speer Library

1 1012 00039 7085

www.ingramcontent.com/pod-product-compliance
Lightning Source LLC
Chambersburg PA
CBHW031814220426
43662CB00007B/636